Carol Hillegas has consolidated very difficult material into an easy and workable tool that can be used personally and globally. During these times of change, I use this body of work that enhances my heart connection with the larger picture of planetary service often. I recommend Carol's work. The Awakened Earth experience will put you in touch with "The Grid of Human Consciousness" and the importance of these times on planet earth.

—Barbra Dillenger, Msc.D
Founder of "The School of Metanoia"

I can attest that Awakened Earth works! It happens exactly in the manner executed and at the precise time executed, creating an environmental change that is rare. Clearly and loudly AE works.

—Bill Drake

The Awakened Earth process has shown me how to work directly with the Masters and Mother Earth. The steps given have created a direct way of interacting. This overall process is easily understood. I have experienced instant results using the AE processes. For me, I can see a new way of communicating with nature. This is the next step in our working together for the good of all.

—Linda Cooper

The possibilities of the Awakened Earth processes are endless. You can work as a group, or individually, on the planet, cosmos, organizations, and the physical body. I have used this process in my personal life with great results. The satisfaction of this non-hierarchal, co-creative process with the Awakened Earth Masters was a deeply rich experience. It is a profound and easy tool to make a difference in these ever-changing times.

—Jackee Earnest

We Are Not Alone
in Our Desire to Heal the Earth

Just because we can't see them does not mean that there are not real and powerful resources available to assist us in bringing our planet back into balance. Carol Hillegas has developed a new model to contact the invisible spiritual forces that are dedicated to planetary healing, and she offers methods of co-creating with them for the greater good of our earth and ourselves.

The Partnership

Doing the work described in *The Awakened Earth* unites three distinct partners: human beings, nature forces often described as devas, and a specific group of spiritual Ascended Masters who identify themselves as the Awakened Earth Masters.

The Process

Following a step-by-step methodology, participants, regardless of their prior knowledge of nature or spiritual principles, are guided in contacting the unseen partners and identifying what is needed to balance a specific environment. This can include working with color infusions, geometric shapes, or frequencies of sound.

Make no mistake about it; while the tools may appear unorthodox, the means of determining their use and applying them is well grounded in scientific method.

The Product

Participants in the Awakened Earth project report observable changes in conditions ranging from desired temperature stabilization to restoration of optimal rainfall. These results can be traced to cause and effect of Awakened Earth efforts. An additional benefit is that as harmony is restored to individual environments, there will be an increase in the balance and health of earth.

For those who have some awareness of the concepts presented in *The Awakened Earth*, the possibilities of applying this new model for global healing are breathtaking. For skeptics, here is an opportunity to challenge and test out something non-traditional and see for yourself whether it is real. For anyone with an open mind and a willingness to take action locally and impact globally, exciting new possibilities await you.

We no longer need to be spectators as pollution and abuse destroy much of the earth, over which we have been given stewardship. We can move from dreaming of a solution to being a significant part of one.

About the Author

Carol Hillegas has been working for many years in cooperation with nature and under guidance from the Awakened Earth Masters. Though she found a fascination with the invisible realm when in her thirties, initially she was reticent to discuss it. But a debilitating illness virtually forced her to turn to these resources for survival. As she recovered—motivated by her passion to help the environment—  Carol applied her healing experience and her own inquiring nature to developing practical, scientifically verifiable ways for anyone to co-create with these unseen but not unknowable forces. The result is the Awakened Earth project and her book *The Awakened Earth*.

Carol is a consultant, speaker, and seminar leader. She lives with her husband, Jim, in Asheville, North Carolina.

The
Awakened Earth

The
Awakened Earth

**A New Model for Co-Creating with Nature and
Other Unseen Forces to Heal Our Planet**

Carol Hillegas

Masters House Press

Asheville, North Carolina

Masters House Press
P. O. Box 5414
Asheville, NC 28813
Phone: 828-505-2102
www.AwakenedEarth.com

Library of Congress Control Number: 2010906964

Publisher's Cataloguing-in-Publication

Hillegas, Carol.

The awakened earth / Carol Hillegas. -- 1st ed. -- Asheville, NC : Master's House Press, 2010.

p. ; cm.

ISBN: 978-0-9845568-0-9
Subtitle on cover: A new model for co-creating with nature and other unseen forces to heal our planet.

1. Geobiology--Philosophy. 2. Earth--Environmental aspects.
3. Ascended masters. 4. Devas. 5. Spiritual life. 6. Healing. I. Title.

QH343.4 .H55 2010   2010906964
508/.01|222   1009

Book Consultant: Ellen Reid
Cover Design: Ghislain Viau
Interior Book Design: Ghislain Viau
Author Photo: Rich Winslow
Editing: Pamela Guerrieri

*This book is dedicated to the many life forms
who will live in harmony and health as a result
of this coming together of humans with the angels.*

Table of Contents

Section Two: After the Awakened Earth Movement Begins

Appendices

Foreword

I wish to share with you my excitement surrounding the ability that each of us has to help in the creation of harmony and balance for Mother Earth and her inhabitants. As I review the last forty years of my life, three most important pieces of information jump out at me:

The first is The Kyron writings. I have been part of this profound, channeled information for the last twenty years. This work helps support the information regarding the shifting of the earth's magnetic grids and our consciousness, enabling us to evolve with ease and grace.

Second is the awareness of the arrival of the Indigo Children *en masse*, with their contract to help positive evolution on Mother Earth. As the Indigos wait for their syllabus, we can feel the shift of vibration that is preparing for their work.

Third, and most important for *now*, is the Awakened Earth project. This information is showing us specific ways to actually co-create, with *The Awakened Earth*, a sustainable environment for our planet.

The last five years have offered me the privilege of working with Carol Hillegas and the Awakened Earth (AE) team. During this time, I realized that we can release any and all forms of victimization regarding earth changes. Even better than this, we can learn how to co-create with the AE, with the goal of harmony and balance—a win-win for all.

Working with Carol and the team, and this information, I have learned how to accurately support the earth. I've experienced many so-called miracles, from watching winds shift within the devastating southern California fires where I live, to learning that animals are beginning to return to the cape of South Africa—including Botswana and the surrounding areas—after they had surprisingly vanished.

Miracles? Yes! It's our birthright to have them ... harmony and balance are natural occurrences to an Awakened Earth and an awakened heart. Thank you, Carol and the AE masters, for clarifying and assisting us with the most important *next step!*

Namaste,
Jan Tober
Co-author of Indigo Children series

Message from the Author

Over the many years that I have worked with nature and the Masters, I have never been as excited as I am now. Environments are changing. They are becoming more balanced, gaining a measure of stability not present before the introduction of the Awakened Earth methods. In today's scenario, we have before us an unparalleled opportunity to assist the earth, and in doing so to assist ourselves. It is no accident that this methodology is being made available in these extraordinary times. You will discover a work of art within The Awakened Earth as you delve into the pages of this co-creative endeavor.

My experience with the co-creative process has evolved over time. When I was first introduced to the unseen world of devas,* I was neither prepared nor capable of communicating with this unseen phenomena. Nature has been my teacher in many aspects of co-creation. As I have grown in my understanding, I also have come to appreciate the depth and knowledge of my unseen partners. They have been with me for more than twenty years, during which time I have marveled at their ability to train me. Much of the learning process involved an in-depth course in letting go. Gradually, as I did so, my co-creative experience gained momentum. The opportunities before me

---

* A deva is a representative of nature and is capable of communicating its intelligence.

began to multiply as I handed over the reins to the higher intelligence I worked in partnership with. Without this relinquishment, I would never have known the co-creative process as it is today.

It is important to note that the "voice" that brings us The Awakened Earth *is that of the Ascended Masters. They will hence be referred to as the Awakened Earth Masters. The material contained in this book was given to me over a period of years. My voice will be in italics. Chapter One is entirely in italics as I deliver my background story. The beginning of Chapter Two continues in my voice until the Awakened Earth Masters pick up where I leave off to become the primary voice throughout the rest of the book. Throughout the book I have inserted some of my thoughts as an adjunct to the voice of the Awakened Earth Masters.*

As you read The Awakened Earth, *realize that you are entering a classroom of unprecedented change. This work is the by-product of my efforts to use co-creation in every aspect of bringing The Awakened Earth into form. Consider this my invitation into a magical place where miracles are commonplace.*

Message from
the Awakened Earth Masters

It is with great honor that this book is presented to you at this time of great change. It has been conclusively demonstrated that the Awakened Earth processes will provide the way for environments to become balanced. As these environments are brought into sustainability and health, the earth will find balance.

The Awakened Earth has been in development for several years. The material has undergone many changes over the course of its coming to you in its present form. Within each chapter are the seeds for transformation. Furthermore, this model is designed to be used by ordinary people in extraordinary times. As you delve into the pages of the book, be prepared to learn many unusual things.

The Awakened Earth will introduce you to a form of co-creation that is a simpler, more direct approach. As a result, it proves more efficient than previous presentations using co-creation as a means to bring information to humanity. We reveal a process by which you may gain insight and a method to reverse years of degradation to the environment. It is certain to offer you the chance to experience an arena of thought not often sought for solutions to perplexing problems. Consider it a path to follow that will help you establish far-reaching and in-depth solutions to many of earth's environmental challenges.

The book has within it the methods and the format for you to become proficient in co-creative partnerships. It also provides the way forward into the era of unification. Unity is at the foundation of *The Awakened Earth*, for unity is the standard for the new world. Gone is separation; in its place is a unifying force called Light. Light possesses a responsibility to deliver unity into environments using the tools provided by *The Awakened Earth*.

As *The Awakened Earth* was coming into form, several things occurred. First, there was a need for this co-creative endeavor to be fully supported by the angelic hierarchy so that whatever was to spring forth would be in alignment with the highest available support in the unseen world. This meant that the hierarchy would ensure that the material in *The Awakened Earth* was aligned with the natural order. Second, there was a need for the project to be elevated to a caliber consistent with the laws of the natural world. To do this, the hierarchy decided to assign four overseers to bring the project to the world. These overseers will remain with the project throughout the entirety of its manifestation.

When the idea for a more balanced earth was first conceived, there was a school of thought that co-creative measures were unsuitable for great expanses of the environment. This concept proved to be erroneous. What follows in this book is a brand new model of co-creation that has exceeded our expectations and has opened the door to a partnership with nature and the Ascended Masters. As this body of work emerged, for the purpose of bringing balance to distressed environments, it became apparent to us that this project was, in fact, creating new pathways for the environment to rejuvenate naturally. Each environment was illustrating a new balance, which gave us the opportunity to assess the Awakened Earth processes in several different environments. What we concluded was that the Awakened Earth processes were a viable means to deliver substantive results. It became clear that we were on to something qualitatively different. We realized that the earth had the ability to reorganize itself in a manner that was new.

Soon after introducing these processes to the Florida coastlines, the land began to come into a new balance. The dunes began to grow grass where there had been none before. Birds long absent began to return. The sand, whose quality had deteriorated, began to revitalize. Evidently, the earth was responding to the influx of harmonious energy delivered through the Awakened Earth processes. We took note. Eventually, along with nature, we came to the conclusion that these processes held within them a secret: balance. This balance, when inserted using these new methods, had the power to rejuvenate large bodies of land and water. Thus, the Awakened Earth was born.

As the co-creative project continued to take shape, we were unsure how to implement such a grand plan for the earth, yet we understood the impact such an endeavor might have. Gradually, as the processes were developed and engaged, we saw firsthand the impact they were having. In addition to Florida, we witnessed an influx of rain to the aquifers of Southern California. We observed that the soil of the land burned in the San Diego County fires, which received the benefit of the Awakened Earth processes and began a process of healing not witnessed before. In 2008, Hurricane Gustav behaved in a manner not seen before. The water has aligned itself with elements that can alleviate massive flooding and has begun to incorporate a more refined balance. This event further confirmed the ability of the Awakened Earth processes to deliver the substantive energy necessary for the earth to come into balance. As we witness more and more of the effects of these new world energies, we are convinced there is reason for great hope.

Since 2004, the Florida coastline has remained stable and has continued to remain in balance. These claims are reinforced by the absence of a devastating hurricane since 2004. Yes, there have been harmful storms, but they have not been as destructive as the storms of 2004 and 2005. There has been harm to some areas, such as the barrier islands along Florida's southernmost beaches, but they have not produced the devastation that came from the series of hurricanes in 2004 and 2005. We attribute this fact to the delivery of energy that is balanced and contains the ingredients for stability. What this tells us is that the likelihood for future devastation will be considerably reduced if these Awakened Earth processes are implemented with regularity. There has not been a significant disturbance in the hurricane corridor since 2005, with the singular exception of Hurricane Ike. (The hurricane corridor includes the Atlantic Basin, the Caribbean, and the Gulf of Mexico.) Yet disturbances have continued in areas that have not received the benefit of the Awakened Earth processes.

In 2005, significant Awakened Earth work was done along the Gulf Coast to the areas impacted by Katrina. Since that time, this area has begun to come into balance. No Awakened Earth processes have been implemented to the area impacted by

Katrina since 2005. We have observed the entire Gulf and its coastline, and we are even more convinced of the practicality of these processes to deliver amazing results.

As we come to understand the breadth and scope of these processes, it is apparent to us that the answer lies in a willingness to construct partnerships dedicated to increasing balance throughout the natural world. In time, we expect there will be changes in the way some of the treated environments respond. What this means to you, the reader, is that you hold the answer in your hands. The Awakened Earth project is the most extensive, co-creative endeavor to be developed for environments. This project comes to you with the blessing of Masters who have been assigned to this work on behalf of earth and humanity. Therefore, you can be assured that the information contained in *The Awakened Earth* is appreciably sound.

What began as an endeavor to help single environments come into balance has, in fact, become a vehicle for the earth to come into balance. Given that we are in a race against time, we urge the readers of this material to be cognizant of the opportunity before them. Never before has a program of such far-reaching potential been presented to humanity. Therefore, we are proposing that those of you reading the material give careful consideration to joining this effort.

The Awakened Earth project has the potential to reverse decades of abuse and mismanagement because it presents a new level of co-creation by engaging "the unseen"—both the body of consciousness known as nature and ourselves, the Awakened Earth Masters. Each of us holds a vibration compatible with humanity that gives us the ability to communicate with you.

In other words, the unseen will join humanity in a co-creative partnership to implement these processes.

As the Awakened Earth model provides the methods to actively assist environments to come into harmony and balance, there will be an upsurge in the way nature and humanity come together. This project will give the reader the ability to work directly with nature and the Awakened Earth Masters.

The earth is vitally invested in the likelihood that the Awakened Earth project will help the planet regain its health and, therefore, its stability. The next thrust for humanity will be in the field of co-creation, which provides a new support system to meet challenges and brings a new arena of thought into the consciousness. This co-creative model stands alone in its capacity to balance and strengthen environments across the globe.

We have dedicated ourselves to bringing forward this extraordinary program. In the pages of this book, you will find protocols never before presented. The Awakened Earth model is different from previous co-creative formulas. The Awakened Earth Masters and nature are here to serve you and allow you to take care of the earth.

This project will set the bar for all future co-creative endeavors. Ultimately, we expect that the Awakened Earth project will take its place in history as a seismic shift in consciousness. As we witness the developments around the world, we are mindful that this project is a beacon to light the way into the future. Those of you who are fortunate enough to be aware of its existence have the key to a future built on principles of balance, stability, and hope. The way is given to you. The rest is up to you.

As we attempt to bring together a clear and dynamic protocol, we face the extraordinary challenge of restructuring all systems and organizing principles. By design, these times are in flux; therefore, any new model—such as the Awakened Earth model— also is continually in flux. We give you this information so that you will be patient; there will be times of great accomplishment and times of unprecedented difficulty. Nevertheless, we are certain you will find this material to be superior and workable, regardless of the outer circumstances.

The Ascended Masters

The Awakened Earth Movement Begins

CHAPTER 1

My Entry into
Partnership with Nature

T he beginnings of my relationship with nature were a surprise
to me. Never in my history had I considered conversing
with the unseen forces of nature—yet this is exactly what
happened. Somewhere along the line, I discovered that the invisible
world held previously unimagined possibilities.

This partnership began when I was introduced to the "nature
kingdoms" by a fellow whose workshop I attended. As he gave an
account of the living spirits in nature—he explained to nature his
need of firewood to heat his farmhouse for the winter. In doing so,
he fully expected the nature kingdoms to comply. He said he simply
asked nature to identify the trees he could fell to give him wood for
the winter. By morning, when the man went into the woods to begin
chopping down trees, he found them already felled. He told us he cut
and stacked the wood, and it turned out to be the exact amount of
wood he needed for the winter! Now I was impressed.

This story kindled a reservoir of knowing I held deep within me. Somehow, I knew there was an intelligence that lived among us. After the workshop, I set out to learn about the nature spirits for myself. My desire to learn about nature took me to Perelandra Nature Research Center, where I had the privilege of meeting Machaelle Small Wright, who has devoted her life to a partnership with such nature intelligences. Upon hearing her speak, I was mesmerized. I wanted to learn more. And so began my journey to learn about and work with these masterful beings.

At the time, my husband and I were considering moving to the mountains of western Virginia, which we did later that same year. In Virginia, while we were building a retreat and conference center, my schooling with nature began. I had the advantage of many hours of solitude in which to build a relationship with nature. As I went through the hands-on experience of creating the retreat center, I learned to rely on nature's help in many aspects of the construction process.

I developed a keen sense of listening within myself for the information I needed. Once, when I was trying to determine the location for the main lodge, I followed nature's lead and let the devas show me the best location. The place they indicated was far superior to our original location. Nature placed the lodge with a mountain view and an ample water supply. I hadn't even considered the water.

Gradually, I turned to nature more and more. Their decisions proved to be far more advantageous than the decisions we made without them. It was as if we had tapped into a resource that was far more capable than we were. For example, when we were having difficulty deciding where to put the road, I asked nature for help. We had been stumbling along with our vision until we realized we were making the project harder than it needed to be. The more I consulted nature, the better things went. Nature had far more wisdom than we had, so we came to rely on nature's intelligence to guide us.

Following this introduction to nature, I began to experiment with more refined issues. I found I was drawn to the environment. I wanted to understand how to clear and balance the energies in environments. Nature schooled me. Together, in a co-creative partnership, nature and I cleared the seventy-seven acres of our retreat center. The benefits were extraordinary: some visitors noticed the purity of the land, while others said they could feel "something different" at the retreat center. I, of course, was delighted to get this unsolicited feedback. It told me something significant was underway. From there, I branched out to clear and balance other properties and businesses.

A chiropractor asked me to clear her office, using the methods I was learning. The next day, her receptionist quit! "Uh-oh," I thought, "I goofed." But the doctor later informed me that the receptionist had not been in alignment with her business. Since hiring a new receptionist, her business was beginning to flourish. This gave me the confidence to try other clearings.

Successes began to build. With nature's help, I removed toxic gas from a property whose inhabitants had gotten sick from the underground fumes. Local officials, who had been contacted, came out to take a look. By the time they got there, not only were the toxic fumes gone, but so was the black sludge that the owner had witnessed accumulating underground. The officials were baffled, but I was thrilled! I was gathering evidence that, by working with nature, we could do the "impossible."

I then moved on to more complex issues. As word spread of my ability to clear and balance environments, I received calls from other places. A woman in Florida was referred to me because she had *been severely poisoned some years earlier. She could no longer live in her home, so she called me to help out. Nature and I treated her home for many months, addressing every nook and cranny on the property. When we were finished, the client and her husband, who were medical doctors, moved back into their home and were able to live there without harm.*

This spawned my deep interest in bringing environments back to health. I pursued this interest for several years until it became evident to me that the earth itself was having difficulty remaining healthy. I asked my unseen partners if we could develop a way to help larger portions of the planet. Surprisingly, they told me "no." I persisted. Gradually, nature and I developed the information that follows in this book.

It has been six years since I first posed that question. In that time, nature and I, along with several Masters who are overseers for the earth, have developed the most extensive program ever to be presented to the earth. This has been no small feat. There have been numerous stumbling blocks. I have had major health issues that slowed me down considerably. My husband and I have moved across the country. Because of my own skepticism, I doubted the possibilities that were emerging. I pressed nature for reliable and substantial results, and soon, they were forthcoming.

Nature and I were in a laboratory of sorts as we sought solutions to a variety of environmental problems. Living in southern California at the time, I was cognizant of the need for water replenishment. And so we began a series of processes to bring the water tables and reservoirs back to health.

Given that these are complex times, the Awakened Earth model is timely and profound. It provides a means for the earth and her environments to come into balance and sustainability. The methods presented here are sound and far-reaching. They will reorder an environment in such a way as to promote healing and, therefore, health. It is impossible to gauge the impact this endeavor will have. Yet I know, firsthand, the miracles I have witnessed as a result of this information.

An Awakened Earth is an earth that is aware of its interconnectedness to all living matter. All living matter benefits from the Awakened Earth model; this has been proven again and again. Now is the time to step into our power as humans and to co-create, with nature and the Masters who are offering their help, the earth we were born to have.

To give you a little of my history, I will open the door to my journey with God. The roots of my spirituality began to form in my mid-thirties. Prior to that time, I had trembled at the thought of God. My childhood included a fearful and punishing God, not someone I would ever turn to for help.

Within the framework of a traditional church, I was given the safety and the structure to form my own beliefs. The church provided me opportunities to explore avenues I had not yet considered. Number one was meditation. I also explored non-traditional ways of being such as learning to appreciate the value of intrapersonal development. The church offered courses of discovery into metaphysics, transpersonal psychology, and leadership development. I gravitated to these more esoteric teachings, while at the same time appreciating the bedrock of Christianity.

In a church Sunday school meditation class, I was introduced to an internal spiritual source I easily identified as Jesus. On the inner planes, Jesus gathered me up, held me close, and promised to lead me out of the wilderness of my fear-filled childhood. And so began a lifelong relationship with "the God of my understanding." I met with Jesus nearly every morning for many years. He trained me, comforted me, and guided me along the "paths of righteousness." As I sought his wisdom, I began to write down his inspiring messages. Nowhere else could I find such personal and uplifting help. Jesus gave me an enduring message of hope while, at the same time, teaching me to trust in a loving being.

Having been deprived of a loving mother, I sought the love of "my Jesus." Jesus never forsook me. He gave me my life and then some. Over time, I capitulated and began to seek God. Given my history, I was timid in my initial attempts to talk to God. However, God, knowing my history, tenderly and slowly guided my conversations. I opened the door to my heart and offered my trust to this internal loving being. As I grew not only in trust but in knowledge of this inner source of strength, I met a woman who changed my life.

Marty Shane, a renowned spiritual master, guided me more deeply into the realms of God. She was only in my life for two short years before she died, yet her impact was life altering. Because of her, my husband and I located our retreat center in the mountains of Virginia. Marty lived in a small town near the North Carolina border. She was a recluse and did not venture far from her home. Yet many found their way to her door. She instructed my husband and me in how to reach God and other Masters on the inner planes. She also provided me with the knowledge that I was to be a "channel." At the time, I had no idea what that meant. Given my upbringing, I was not aware of these elements of thought. However, with innate wisdom, Marty knew of my capacity for reaching into the larger universe. She gave me the tools to do so. She also schooled me in the ways of the Masters, who were to become my companions. I gained experience and validated my gifts while studying with Marty. Not only did she teach me, but she also provided me the resources to teach myself. She gave me the ability to enter the stillness and sit with God. I learned to listen and discern the voice within. Over time, I have become a clear channel for the God of my understanding.

God lives in my heart. God is my confidante and friend. God speaks to me daily. God has prompted me to write this book. By nature, I am a private person. God plans to change that. I have no idea what lies ahead, but I am certain it will be better than I can imagine. God has never let me down. The fact that this book is becoming a reality is proof of that. I did not set out to write a book, but God did. What you hold in your hand is God's gift. I have been the vessel. No where in my history did I imagine this reality. However, when I turned to God in a time of despair, God took the reins and has led me from that day forward. That day was twenty-five years ago. What follows in the pages of The Awakened Earth is the result of surrendering my life to a power greater than myself.

CHAPTER 2

Nature Begins to Co-Create with Humanity

W hen I first began working with nature, I was ignorant of the ways this work might help humanity. Nevertheless, I was drawn into the world of angelic forces living in the natural world. As this world entered into my awareness, I became fascinated by the possibilities present in the field of co-creation.

I had seen evidence while building the retreat center that convinced me I was in the presence of an intelligent force. As I expanded my view, I was given a chance to witness many other incidents where co-creation was coordinating and manifesting results beyond the norm. Not only had nature assisted with the placement of the lodge, it also gave me the "specs" for a workable garden that flourished with little attention from me and provided sufficient food for a number of retreatants and ourselves. Little did I know that nature was preparing me for a larger role.

In keeping with our intention to work in harmony and balance with the natural world, we were given a chance to learn at the feet of *the masters – the devas and the nature spirits residing at Springwood. I began to intuit a greater role in working with these intelligences. Some of the time these masters of the natural world were physically present. I could feel them all about me. Their energy was light like a feather tickling my skin. At other times I would hear their whispers. As I attuned to their presence, I began to hear their whispers more and more. Not wanting to lose their wisdom, I began to write their messages in a journal. They guided me. They answered my questions. I began to trust them as the information these intelligences were providing was appreciably sound.*

Early on, I was drawn to the environmental processes and to the idea that they could be balanced and, therefore, come into alignment with a higher order. It was a small leap for me to begin to work co-creatively with nature on behalf of environments.

Somehow I knew that there was energy present in the air about me. This energy was a life force that begged to be recognized. It was if the invisible space around me had a message to give me. So I listened and learned this energy was real. Sometimes this energy was stale. Sometimes it was heavy. Sometimes it was light. If a room had been able to talk, I would have known its pain, its sorrow, its past. All of a sudden, I realized that there were differences in the quality of the energy in a room. The energy held memories of those who had been there before. For example, if a traumatic event had occurred, the emotions of that event were still present. As I began to pay attention, I picked up the differences from place to place.

Nature was teaching me that environments held memories that remained long after the event. Based on what I was also learning from the Perelandra Garden Workbook, it seemed to me that environments could be cleared and balanced and, therefore, become a more harmonious field. It was a small leap for me to begin to work in partnership with nature to help environments come into balance.

I began to practice the techniques I was learning from Machaelle Small Wright. It was evident to me that there were significant changes to the environments I was working on. I grew in my confidence and began to share with others some of the techniques I was learning. As word spread, I was called upon to clear and balance farms, homes, businesses, and more. One time when I was clearing a piece of property, I "saw" some horses leaving the property, only to learn from the owner that the property had at one time been a horse farm. Another time I "witnessed" a fire on the property and was told that there had been a massive fire there years before. The pain of the people living there at the time of the fire was still in existence until it was cleared co-creatively by nature and me. These experiences helped me to realize that environments held energies and that these energies could be transformed.

Soon properties with toxins were presented to me. A friend called me to see if I could remove the smoke from the leather sofas and other furniture in the house they were renting. Her husband was extremely sensitive to smoke and was having difficulty remaining in the house with the smoke-filled furniture. I went to nature and asked if this condition could be treated. Their answer was yes. Together, nature and I were able to bring the house into harmony by removing the smoke. I didn't do it, nature did. I provided the intention and nature came up with the plan. Then I implemented the plan. This work was done before I had even conceived The Awakened Earth. Later when I was considering the best way to use my skills with nature's expertise, I never fully imagined the scope and breadth of what is now possible. I simply had an idea, took it to nature, and together we began to develop a more comprehensive way to address issues on a much larger scale. This is co-creation.

In the beginning of this project when I had no earthly idea of how to bring the project into a workable format, I went to my guidance and asked for their help. By this time, I was not only working with nature, but I was also communicating with other Masters on a regular basis. For me, this is as easy as breathing, and I wanted it to be as easy for others. Considering my love of the environment, it was natural for me to go to my unseen partners and ask for their help. Initially, bringing balance to large environments was thought to be unworkable. However, I persisted. In the spring of 2004, I went to a dear friend, prompted by a nudge from my guidance, and asked her to help me create a program to help environments come into balance. Together we began to develop the first of what was to become the Awakened Earth Processes. To help me in my quest, I asked two other women, equally devoted to serving the earth, to join me. The four of us began to develop the processes we have now.

We met in each others' homes, twice a month, sometimes more, and perfected the new Awakened Earth Processes. This entire endeavor was done by using the co-creative format I am presenting in this book. I called upon the resources of nature and the Ascended Masters to help us. This work continued over the next two years until we felt we had the foundational processes to serve the earth in her time of need. Eventually we produced fifteen processes and administered them to selected environments as a test run. Remarkably these environments began to respond in ways that were new. For example, when southern California experienced several wildfires, we approached nature and the Masters and asked if we could subdue these rampant fires. They agreed and gave us a series of processes to apply to the devastated areas. Without knowing if these processes could help, we were more than willing to try. Not only did the fires subside, but the land that had been burned began to rejuvenate in a way that nature said was more comprehensive than any other methodology currently in existence.

Subsequent to the fires southern California, where I was living at the time was experiencing a severe and prolonged drought. Again, we asked nature if this could be addressed using the processes we were developing. They agreed to give it a try. Remember, nothing remotely similar to this had ever been tried. Yet something in me knew that it was possible. So we ventured forth into an unknown universe, using co-creation to address large areas of drought. We asked nature to help us frame a suitable intention knowing that the intention held the blueprint for co-creation to be fulfilled. We presented our requirements and nature gave us an intention that was aligned with the natural order. This was done by trial and error until we had a statement that our unseen partners were satisfied with. Then we would proceed to ask which of the processes were suitable to fulfill our intention for drought relief in San Diego County. At the time, in 2005, the reservoirs were precariously low. And so began our experimentation. Within a few short weeks, the reservoirs and water tables were coming alive with water. Our nearby Lake Hodges began to fill before our eyes. Before long, the waters were flowing over the top of the gates and spilling into the river below.

It dawned on me that we were on to something remarkable, and yet, I was not ready to proclaim victory. I needed more "proof" before I was willing to give credence to what I was seeing. The other women also were hesitant to believe these processes were capable of such miracles. We continued our bi-monthly meetings and addressed other environmental dilemmas. We usually worked together in our co-creative partnership for two hours. These sessions were easy, uplifting, and filled me with joy. The other women reported similar experiences.

Another issue we addressed was the rampant windstorms that were so injurious to the balance of nature. Locally these are known as the Santa Annas, hot desert winds that dry out the vegetation and prolong the fire season. While we were experimenting, yet another firestorm rolled through San Diego County. We were unable to bring the fire down, but we were able to increase the moisture in the air, which helped the overall ecosystem. Nature told us that future fires would be lessened as a result of the attention San Diego County had received from the processes we were delivering. All of this pointed to a model of co-creation to address large environments and help them to come into greater balance and harmony.

To work more effectively with our unseen partners, I was asked to establish a more comprehensive pendulum format. We had outstripped the "yes" and "no" format I was accustomed to. Thus, the expanded pendulum format was born. Nature had worked with me over the years using the simple "yes/no" format. This time they wanted something more comprehensive so misunderstandings could be minimized. Together we worked out the format I use today. It has given me the wherewithal to create a working environment nothing short of miraculous. We understand each other remarkably well. With the communication piece in place, the Awakened Earth Project was born.

In this book will be a dynamic called co-creation. However, the model of co-creation presented in *The Awakened Earth* is qualitatively different. It is composed of components that bring together in partnership the consciousness of nature and the consciousness of humanity. In this endeavor, we will portray nature in a light that is new.

Nature, by all accounts, has been greatly misunderstood. It is time to set the record straight. As we delve into the truth of nature, we will expose erroneous beliefs. Nature has a consciousness. Nature is capable of co-creating with humanity for the purpose of bringing balance to earth and her environments, which is of great importance, especially during these times of great change.

The Awakened Earth project has been in development for nearly six years. From the perspective of the Awakened Earth Masters, this project is the most significant environmental breakthrough of our time. During the development of the Awakened Earth project, the earth has continued to experience severe alterations to many of its habitats and ecosystems. What follows in this book is a model for reversing years of degradation and neglect to habitats and ecosystems around the world.

The project will be shown to be a model worthy of its name: The Awakened Earth. With the introduction of the Awakened Earth energies comes an enlightening endeavor filled with hope. This endeavor will demonstrate its effectiveness. One cannot come to this project and not be certain of its power to rewrite environmental history.

The Awakened Earth offers the opportunity for humanity to reach beyond its limitations and discover a world without bounds: the world of universal consciousness. In the pages of *The Awakened Earth*, humanity is invited to discover the possibilities of working in partnership with the consciousness of nature and with the Awakened Earth Masters. While this may seem impossible, it is not. Nature is a willing and able partner.

In addition, Masters have been assigned to oversee the Awakened Earth. In keeping with the universal consciousness, the Awakened Earth Masters will bring their wisdom and investment to this project. This deliberate association is your guarantee that the Awakened Earth is authentic. We tell you this to dispel any doubts or misgivings you may have.

The mission of the Awakened Earth is to harness the power of co-creation to fulfill earth's destiny. In addition, this mission will bring light to environments across the globe and, in so doing, bring balance and health. The scope of this mission is without equal.

The Awakened Earth project intends to broaden humanity's reach by interfacing with the consciousness of nature. With the establishment of an intention, the partnership is set into motion. When the human member comes to nature and says, "I wish to join with nature for the purpose of bringing health and sustainability to the woodlands behind my home," nature will automatically align the partnership with the members necessary to fulfill the stated intention. The Awakened Earth Masters will always be a part of each partnership with nature. In this book are the steps and considerations to make this a reality. Nature is equipped to infuse energy into any environment if certain criteria are met. The criteria will be outlined in future chapters.

Within *The Awakened Earth* are seeds of great change, both immediate and far-reaching. It is hoped that this book will create sufficient interest and momentum to alter individual environments and significantly improve environments across the world. We have begun to witness encouraging signs; environments that receive the benefit of the Awakened Earth energies respond in ways never before witnessed.

In the wake of Hurricane Katrina, there has been widespread interest in helping the environment, but other models are failing to bring balance and health to the many challenged environments. The Awakened Earth methods, when employed as presented, will deliver practical solutions to help these environments begin the long road back to health.

It is important to state that we are grateful for this opportunity. The Awakened Earth Masters have been waiting for a time when humanity was ready to merge with the unseen. Given that we are embarking on a new course, it is important that you understand the commitment you are making. Consider your decision carefully. Some of you will be ready to move into full, co-creative partnerships. Others will need some practice in order to gain a working knowledge of how co-creative partnerships function. Some will do best by forming small groups to work with an environment; we would suggest groups of not more than four persons. While establishing these groups, it is important to remember that you may be working together for several months.

The Awakened Earth energies have begun to change the balance in some ecosystems. There have been significant changes to the western North Carolina Mountains, where consistent effort to replenish the aquifers and water tables has resulted in significant rainfall, giving the reservoirs the needed water to flourish. In addition, the overall health and balance have become apparent. There is ample growth of all vegetation and a new balance in the insect population; several insect species have significantly regained their prominence in the ecosystem. The hornets and wasps have been challenged, but with the recent rains, these insects have begun to show signs of recovery. The bee populations have been significantly reduced in recent years; with the moisture returning, we expect the bee population to begin to rebound. As the bees return to the mountains, pollination will increase and more species will come back into balance. This is a positive sign for the overall health of the ecosystem. Without an established balance, an ecosystem can fall into disease and deterioration.

Along the Florida coastlines, there are signs of rejuvenation as the wildlife returns. Flocks of pelicans are now residing along the south Florida inter-coastal waterway, returning to previously vacated habitats. Blue herons are living in the swamp grasses along the shores of Lake Okeechobee, although these birds have not been present there since the early 1970s. Several other species of animals have taken up residence in the low-lying grasses.

Areas that were burned in the 2004 southern California fires have begun to rejuvenate in a way that suggests that the new energies have had an impact; they are recovering quickly. Areas of land burned in 2007 fires that were exposed earlier to Awakened Earth processes also have been rejuvenated. These factors and many others have given us the impetus to bring this work to fruition, so that humanity can begin the long process of rebuilding other environments.

Both natural environments and human-created organizations may benefit from Awakened Earth methodology. There will be appreciable differences in the way individual environments respond to these processes. Some will come into balance with minimal applications, while others will require several insertions of energy. The endeavors best suited for the Awakened Earth model are: the natural environment, organizations with complex systems that are restructuring, and any structure in need of alignment with the natural order. By "natural order," we mean a system of balance governed by the laws in place throughout the natural world. An example of this would be organizational entities that have an inherent consciousness of the higher order.

When humanity comes to the realization that there are new avenues to help solve seemingly unworkable and problematic situations in both natural and manmade arenas, there will be a major influx of interest in co-creative partnerships.

Nature Brings a New Awareness

In times of change, new methods can slip onto the world's stage. The earth is in need of the new solutions to its pressing problems and those solutions are contained within *The Awakened Earth*. In order to establish balance and sustainability on a planet clearly in distress, the Awakened Earth project will establish nature as the dominant partner. Nature is far more than a benign entity; its mission is to bring harmony and balance into every aspect of the natural world. It sees its mission in terms of equality for all life, whether human, animal, plant, or mineral. Nature is NOT a violent or malevolent force, but a consciousness of true balance. In its quest for balance, nature can produce outcomes that appear to be out of balance, in order to establish real balance. Nature also can produce amazing results when working in a co-creative partnership, provided that humanity first sets the intention to do so. Nature is an ally, not an adversary, in this process.

These times have opened the doorway to expansion and greater awareness of living in balance. There has been great change in the way humanity resources information. Until now, it would have been premature to introduce this course to the world, but when it becomes known that nature and humanity are forming functional partnerships to give the earth what she needs, we expect many will want to join the effort.

This project has become more than its original intention; as environments began to rejuvenate, it became apparent to the collective that this work was capable of much more. It then became a simple matter to invest fully in this far-reaching project.

Nature noticed the impact of the new processes. Environments were then selected by a group of dedicated women serving the earth; the common theme in these early endeavors was water replenishment. When the aquifers in southern California were devastatingly low, it was decided to employ the new Awakened Earth processes there; the aquifers began to fill almost immediately. It was then that nature began to take the idea of co-creating with humans seriously and began to develop suitable processes to bring harmony and balance to those environments by employing co-creation, color, higher intelligence, light, energetic formulas of elements aligned with the natural order, sacred geometry, and the Source's energy. Without question, these tools have proven to be effective.

An Opportunity for Co-Creation

The Awakened Earth Masters are Ascended Masters, beings whose mission is to serve the will of God for the betterment of all life. The commitment of these Masters to endorse a project and to oversee it throughout its incarnation is unique. As this project becomes known, it will give direction to helping many other difficulties currently without solution. It is hoped that many fields of study will see the usefulness in co-creation.

As we gathered information through the implementation of the Awakened Earth processes, we knew this model had the capacity to deliver substantive results. Now, as we become aware that the Awakened Earth is subject to an investment by humanity and is in alignment with the overall intention for the earth, we are reminded of the significant opportunity for co-creation to influence the course of history. The intention of the earth is to continue, with humanity, to live in harmony and balance. This intention serves as the foundation for all partnerships, which will carry within them the constructive forces of the higher dimensions.

A co-creative partnership brings together disparate elements for a higher purpose and births an even higher order. In the new order, there will be a synthesis of aspects of harmony and balance that will induce a higher order still. From this higher order comes a gathering of forces intended to bring about a new order. We expect to see a coming together of consciousness that will accelerate the expansion of the earth.

The Awakened Earth Model of Co-Creation

In order to establish a fully functioning co-creative endeavor, the human member brings an intention, which sets the stage for nature to join humanity in a co-creative partnership to fulfill the stated intention. The partnership will come together automatically. You will not have to identify individual members. The appropriate members will join automatically based upon the intention. This is where this model diverges from other models. This co-creative foundation is necessary for all working partnerships.

The Awakened Earth model defines "co-creative partnerships" as a partnership called into being by humanity. The partnership includes three components: a member from the Awakened Earth Masters, a representative from the body of nature, and a human member. This partnership always sets the intention in motion. The goal of this project is to implement the Awakened Earth processes.

It will be important that the partnerships adhere to the principles. The course found in *The Awakened Earth* will provide the earth the assistance needed to achieve greater balance and will support the earth in continuing its journey with humanity. The vision for the Awakened Earth project is to bring balance to environments that have sustained great damage so that the earth can rejuvenate and live cooperatively with humanity.

Several factors must be considered. First, nature wants to work with humanity for the purpose of bringing health to many of earth's damaged environments. Second, nature has come into partnership with individuals who have dedicated themselves to helping secure a more balanced future for the earth. Third, the body of nature has come forward at this time, in order to help the earth and its inhabitants live in harmony and continue their journey together.

The Movement Begins

Once the earth has begun to establish a working balance, it is projected that much of the natural world will be able to function in a state of balance. The earth will begin to experience some shifts throughout its entire body. Once these energies take hold, the earth will function in a more cohesive manner and will begin to hold a new resonance that will alleviate some of the discord that has damaged significant portions of the planet. As this happens, there will be some noticeable changes. The earth will respond and become more balanced.

As humanity and nature move forward in this endeavor, there will be some challenges to overcome. It is possible that some environments will respond differently than hoped for. In this case, nature will have to adjust to the circumstances in whatever ways are indicated at the time. Sometimes additional measures will be needed to allow the environment to come into balance. For example, as we dedicated ourselves to correcting the imbalances in the western North Carolina Mountains, we discovered that we had to also adjust the atmosphere, which contributed to the overall moisture imbalance. Once this atmospheric issue was identified, we were able to implement the Awakened Earth processes more effectively.

The earth has the capacity to come into balance by accepting the energies presented in *The Awakened Earth*. In all likelihood, the earth will make this transition with ease, knowing that these energies are compatible with her needs. Awakened Earth processes will help the earth in its larger role of providing light for the universe.

The Awakened Earth model also will present a new understanding of the co-creative process. The Awakened Earth Masters, along with nature, will need to be understood as a collective intelligence. The unseen is a reliable partner and can be counted upon to correct the imbalances.

The earth is a living, breathing body that has been much misunderstood. This must change. With the introduction of the Awakened Earth processes, the earth already is gaining more momentum and inspiration to align with her own capacity for balance. The earth also has agreed, as part of her evolution, to work with those of you who establish co-creative partnerships.

It is hoped that small groups will form to address specific environments that have been deteriorating for decades. This project, when fully launched, will allow for many environments to recalibrate and come into a more suitable state of equilibrium. Gradually, as the impact of the Awakened Earth spreads across the globe, there will be recognition that something magnificent is underway. Nature and humanity will provide the lifeline to reestablish balance. Indeed, there is no time to lose.

The earth can and will achieve balance. The question has always been whether the earth and humanity can achieve balance together. The earth has never before worked together with humanity for this purpose, and in the short term, it may experience some growing pains as it relies upon these processes to help.

For many years now, I have desired to support the earth in a way that could make a difference in the lives of people. Never could I have imagined a comprehensive program with the power to effect change to environments across the world— yet that is what this program offers. I hope to illustrate the power of the Awakened Earth co-creative partnerships to change the way we live without disturbing the natural order. This model of co-creation does this because it is in alignment with the natural order. It gives humanity the ability to direct its future in a way that is self-sustaining. What you can imagine can become reality. Dream big! You may be pleasantly surprised.

What the Awakened Earth Is

In earlier times, the earth was considered a planet of unlimited resources. However, as the population has grown, it has become apparent that much of the natural world is in crisis. As the world comes to understand the correlation between cause and effect, it can recognize that much of the natural world is having difficulty maintaining balance. Because the earth is challenged by the demands made upon its natural resources, there has been a need to conserve. But it also has become necessary to address the imbalances caused by an apparent lack of understanding with regard to how the earth remains in balance.

The earth is having difficulty keeping alignment with its overall intent to live in harmony with humanity, which is a prerequisite for the earth to become self-sustaining. This, of course, can happen if sufficient numbers are made aware of the consequences of disregarding nature as an integral part of humanity. As it gradually becomes common knowledge that humanity and nature are intricately linked, there can be a reversal of the degradation ruining much of the planet. Nature has within her the ability to rejuvenate, but only if humanity comes to terms with the interconnectedness of all life. Nature can directly influence how the earth regains balance and sustainability.

The Awakened Earth is a balanced earth that recognizes its interconnectedness with all living matter. As the earth begins to incorporate the new energies, provided by the Awakened Earth and its participants, it will begin to achieve the inner balance that is a prerequisite for all environments to be in harmony. The balanced earth can strengthen and harmonize individual environments, and as it gains momentum from the Awakened Earth processes, it will experience more balance than ever before. The earth is relying on the generosity of humanity to take responsibility for setting these processes in motion.

We have noticed that whenever the Awakened Earth processes are engaged, there is an immediate increase in the amount of Light. Light is the aggregate accumulation of beneficial energies inserted into any given environment. Light brings balance and balance brings harmony. Light is deposited in such a way that an environment can readily accept it. In this way, the earth can begin to realize its potential for balance. As the earth begins its journey into a higher state of consciousness, it will have to rely on humanity to broaden its support using the Awakened Earth model of co-creation.

Earth is, by nature, a planet of self-sufficiency. No other planet has this capacity for rejuvenation. Once the Awakened Earth energies, as described in this book, are introduced into an environment, there are a number of changes that begin to take place. First, the environment takes on characteristics that are unique to its expression as a life form and that bring it back into a state of harmony and viability.

The collective life form will have to adjust to the changes the Awakened Earth energies create. Once the environment has come to integrate the benefits of such changes, it becomes new-actually, it returns to its original state of balance. As the entire ecosystem comes into a state of harmony, the environment will take on characteristics necessary for on-going balance.

There are safeguards built into the Awakened Earth processes. The Awakened Earth Masters will not allow implementation of the Awakened Earth processes to any environment unless the partnership is in alignment with the highest good. Many of you have come to this work from other forms of co-creation, but these forms, while useful, are not the same as the Awakened Earth process. To participate in the Awakened Earth assumes responsibility and an acknowledgement that the earth is our host and should be respected and cared for as one would care for a family member. In keeping with the natural laws, the Awakened Earth can be relied upon to be in integrity.

The unseen forces of nature can and will restore any environment in jeopardy, as long as humanity comes and asks for help. It is that simple. Decades-old deteriorations can be reversed, as long as the Awakened Earth model is engaged with integrity. To responsibly address the many issues facing the environment at this time in history is monumental. Timeliness is crucial for the earth to come into balance.

The earth has had to adjust to the many challenges brought about by man's exploitation and has had to endure flagrant abuse. Humanity has destroyed many of the rainforests and hastened the drying up of rivers, lakes, and aquifers across the land. It has also witnessed some of the most devastating storms ever recorded. And yet, humanity continues to deny her role in these monumental changes. Look around you. Everywhere there is evidence of neglect of the earth, yet most of humanity chooses to ignore it. How long do you think this can continue? Will you join in this monumental effort to help the earth?

Those with access to power and influence have led you to believe that global warming is not a threat. It is. The earth can no longer sustain a balanced state without human intervention. What is needed for earth and humanity to move forward together is a shift in consciousness that allows a new paradigm to emerge. The earth is ready and willing to partner with humanity in an attempt to bring balance into the many deteriorating environments. Earth has the capacity to withstand these imbalances, but only if humanity takes up the banner and begins to implement the Awakened Earth model. We are giving you facts. Are you willing to make the commitment to the earth? Are you willing to form co-creative partnerships to do so?

The Earth Is Changing

The earth has begun to develop new ways of adjusting to the influx of energy from the Awakened Earth. The earth recognizes the energy and incorporates it into the overall life force. However, the earth is having a difficult time adjusting to the depletion of her resources. Much of the deforestation has depleted the earth's ability to accommodate the breadth of humanity currently residing upon her. In the span of forty years, the earth has lost her ability to function in balance. In order to come back into balance, the earth must partner with humanity in co-creative partnerships. The formula for these partnerships is presented in the following chapters of *The Awakened Earth*. In this world of cause and effect, there are consequences for ignoring the reality of humanity's contribution to the failure to co-exist with the earth.

To enter into a co-creative partnership of this magnitude requires a recognition that we all are in this together. This model has, at its core, cooperation between nature and humanity. It has no other agenda than bringing balance and harmony to earth. Those of you joining this project will find yourselves with an opportunity of unprecedented learning. Because the Awakened Earth model of co-creation is a conduit for energies from higher dimensions, when you engage the Awakened Earth model, you will be bringing a higher vibration into environments across the world. This will open the gates for environments to be aligned with the vibrations needed to further the balance, and ultimately the evolution, of the earth.

As these processes were introduced into environments, the amount of Light increased. As the Light increased, the environments began to coalesce around a higher order. Nature was astonished, as this had never been witnessed before. This gave nature information that allowed nature to understand that the harmonious energy was contributing to the increase in the Light quotient. With this realization, nature was able to conclude that these processes had potential. It became apparent that something significant was underway.

As this realization became evident, nature knew the Awakened Earth had the capacity to deliver significant results. Furthermore, once it became evident that this co-creative model could serve as the foundation for future partnerships, nature championed the Awakened Earth wholeheartedly. Because the Awakened Earth Masters and nature have agreed to serve humanity, and this endeavor serves humanity and the earth, it was concluded that the Awakened Earth would serve the greater good while serving humanity. The Awakened Earth Masters also concluded that, once this material was available to the general population, it would help humanity with the understanding that an invisible, cooperative force could join with humanity to bring about productive change.

Using this model of co-creation, the earth already has begun to reverse some significant deterioration. With the introduction of these higher level energies, the earth is coming into a new vibration. As more environments are the beneficiaries of this productive energy, the earth will continue to change. As the vibrations continue to shift and expand, it is expected that the earth will come into greater and greater balance.

CHAPTER 3

Nature and Its Bounty

As time went on, I realized that the focus of the Awakened Earth was to create a deliberate method to bring balance into previously neglected environments. This meant that, for the first time, humanity and nature would be partnering for the purpose of aligning environments with a higher order. It also meant that we would be constructing a means to address issues that had never been addressed co-creatively before. At first, I was reluctant to expect this undertaking to have measurable results. However, since I was having some success with nature in addressing my complex health issues, I felt it was worth the try.

As I said earlier, the women's group I had put together was having some success with issues in Southern California. I wanted to expand my horizons and take this work to a new level. Once I made the decision to develop programs specifically designed to help larger environments, I became more aware of global weather patterns. Some of the issues that struck me were weather related and causing considerable damage. One such issue was the hurricanes pounding

Florida. In my mind I questioned, was it possible to minimize the damage these hurricanes were causing? I asked nature. Nature indicated there was a possibility that some of the damage could be lessened by introducing some of the newly developed processes. That was all I needed to hear. I wanted to help. Now perhaps I could.

Nature and I began a series of treatments to help bring balance into the area where the hurricanes were developing. I tracked the hurricanes through the Caribbean and into the Gulf of Mexico, applying some of the processes available to me at the time. We had limited success. The hurricanes diminished in intensity but still struck the land, causing considerable damage. Undeterred, I pursued the hurricanes throughout the season. Evidently nature was gathering data and devising new means to address hurricanes. Several new processes were developed, bringing the total to fifteen. At the time there were just ten. So the seeds were planted. Gradually as the Awakened Earth began to take root, I held out hope that eventually we could more effectively address hurricanes. Nature indicated there was the possibility that something could be done down the road. I also held onto my hope that drinking water could be made potable. As of now, water is still on my wish list. Eventually, as new processes come on line, it may become a reality. And so I venture on, determined to realize my dream that clean, pure water can someday become a reality.

As the project was beginning to take shape, the Awakened Earth Masters were taking notice of the results in Southern California. Suddenly, it was as if there was an opportunity growing, in the midst of a very dry climate, to bring water into the reservoirs and aquifers. Early on, it had been considered impossible to bring balance to extensive bodies of land. Nevertheless, it was becoming a reality, as the reservoirs and aquifers began to fill. Slowly, we began to take seriously the capacity for co-creation to bring balance and equip environments to become self-sustaining.

What has emerged is a program that contains within it the seeds for great change. What is more, when delivered correctly, the Awakened Earth processes are irrefutably sound. The combination of Awakened Earth processes and the delivery system of co-creation are the most effective means ever known to mankind. In other words, what is contained in the pages of the Awakened Earth has the potential to change the course of history.

As we come to terms with the possibility that the earth can successfully come into balance, using the Awakened Earth methods gives us the impetus for writing this book. These methods will offer solutions to a wide range of environmental difficulties. Some situations that can be addressed using the Awakened Earth model are: restoration of aquifers and reservoirs; rejuvenation of wetlands; soil replenishment along storm-ravaged coastlines; continued replenishment of water to drought-stricken areas; ongoing management of heat and humidity; and restoration of habitats that have been destroyed during hurricanes. These, and many more conditions, can be reversed.

The areas that have been treated with the Awakened Earth measures have begun to show signs of rejuvenation. As more and more evidence has been gained, we have become convinced that environmental changes are taking place. This has given us the impetus to come up with a program that could be implemented using the dynamic of co-creation.

We have been striking out in uncharted territory. Never before have we considered co-creation as a means to deliver balance to environments. Nevertheless, we have discovered, quite by accident, that co-creation offers a most suitable means for delivering the necessary ingredients for environments to be infused with viable means of rejuvenation. This investigation gave us the opportunity to look at how environments have been responding to the influx of necessary ingredients for rejuvenation.

These partnerships will have the capacity to reverse many of the long-standing environmental issues facing humanity. As we have indicated earlier, the Awakened Earth measures can and will reverse decades of abuse and misunderstanding.

These processes have the potential to bring about significant improvement to a host of other situations as well. Some additional situations that can be helped by using the Awakened Earth model are as follows: rebalancing the individual environments along waterways impacted by development, ongoing support for environments that have been subjected to earth erosion, and restoration of habitats along storm tracks. These and many other environmental conditions can be helped by using the Awakened Earth processes.

Given that we are entering a time of unprecedented change, we will need to develop measures that will increase the likelihood for the environment to be cared for in a manner that is consistent with co-creative philosophy. When this happens, more groups such as this co-creative endeavor will begin to form. We are establishing a new level of understanding that will carry humanity forward for years to come.

New methods are needed to address the deterioration of environments throughout the world. Balance is the underlying condition necessary for environments to become viable. As you may have gathered, we are entering a world that will bring humanity into contact with a larger field of consciousness.

The methods we will be using will include co-creative partnerships, energy transference, and a willingness to set aside preconceptions. As we turn the page into the new world, we will move from human-centered applications to co-creative solutions. Human beings will need time to become capable of working effectively with the unseen. As we proceed with this endeavor, there will be some of you ready to move into full, co-creative partnerships. Others of you will need some practice in order to gain a working knowledge of how co-creative partnerships function.

Much of what we will teach you will be new information. This work, while similar to other forms of co-creation, is unique. As you gain an understanding of the overall intent of this work, you will appreciate the differences. As we equip you with this new way to bring balance into environments, we will give you measures to work with that are different from other forms of co-creation.

We are aware that some of you have been working in facsimiles of co-creative partnerships. However, the Awakened Earth partnerships are qualitatively different. In our partnerships, there is a collective energy created by an intention. The intention serves to bring together the components of nature necessary for fulfilling the stated intention. As the intention is fulfilled, nature and humanity agree to adhere to the natural laws of the universe. For example, in the case of the California wildfires, there has been a reconfiguring of the soil's composition to indicate that the utilization of these processes has prepared the soil in a way that supports revitalization and rejuvenation. Without this method of co-creation, this re-composition would not have been achieved.

We have witnessed significant change along the western portion of California. The recent fires have initiated a rebirth of vegetation, which, in turn, has spawned the birth of other vegetation not present for many decades. An example of this is the resurgence of grasses, which have the capacity to enrich the soil and make it resistant to future destabilization. While there has been progress in rebuilding the soil's composition, there also has been an influx of foreign matter, as the result of indigenous species becoming stronger and developing safeguards to protect their survival. The foreign matter comes in to help the host species develop stronger root systems, in order to maintain their integrity.

The Consciousness Has Shifted

There can be no doubt that you are participating in the most far-reaching endeavor ever to be presented in the human forum. Therefore, be assured that you have opened the pathways to a new existence. Contained within the Awakened Earth model are principles that have never before been introduced to humanity. It is a given that this work will generate more change than anything presented to humanity before.

Since the initial launch of this project, there has been a remarkable shift in the overall consciousness, which has allowed for this work to begin taking its place in the larger framework of global consciousness. There has been an increase in understanding of the interrelatedness of all living beings on the earth. Earth has assumed an active role in coming to terms with the larger shift in consciousness. Furthermore, earth has begun to accept the energies present in each of the Awakened Earth processes. What this means to those of you reading this material is that you now have the tools to return significant balance to environments across the globe. In addition, you can influence the outcomes of many of the earth's jeopardized environments.

As you engage with the processes presented in the Awakened Earth, you will be at the leading edge of the environmental movement. Furthermore, you will have the opportunity to expand your own consciousness as you interact with the many forces of nature joining you in this momentous project. We stand ready to join you in this magnificent endeavor on behalf of all life. As you become involved in this co-creative endeavor, you are apt to recognize the impact you are having to environments that, until now, have been deteriorating. This project is the work of a few who have seen the potential and have waited for this moment to bring hope and inspiration to a world that has nearly lost its hope. As the news of the Awakened Earth becomes known, we expect many will want to become involved in bringing balance to the earth.

We have the utmost faith in the work we are presenting here. If you choose to become involved, you will be contributing to a larger movement to allow the earth to become the light she is meant to be. In this role, earth will provide the light for the entire universe, so that as the earth transitions to a higher resonance, there will be sufficient momentum to carry the entire universe. This will alleviate any measure of conjecture on the part of humanity as to the importance of light in bringing earth into alignment with her designated role.

The Awakened Earth will assist the earth in becoming stable and capable of maintaining stability throughout these changing times. The energy available in the Awakened Earth processes will accumulate and give the earth the boost she needs to move into her rightful position as the light force for the entire universe. The earth has agreed to be this guiding light force.

Once these energies are introduced into environments across the globe, some situations to be addressed will require extra balance. In the case of western North Carolina, there is an ongoing effort to maintain balance through ongoing maintenance. The western North Carolina region has been experiencing some pertinent rejuvenation as the result of the ongoing maintenance of its ecosystem. Once it is realized that the Awakened Earth methods can be utilized in many different environments, we expect an increased emergence in co-creation.

The Function of Co-Creative Science

Nature is a balance of many elements, which are always in motion. With the influx of higher-dimensional energies, we have come to understand the importance of working with humanity so that the overall balance of an environment can be addressed through co-creative means. Broadly speaking, there are components of co-creation that have the ability to move beyond conventional science. Science has always provided the means to equip humanity with the understanding necessary to offer a cohesive and deliberate hypothesis. Now, however, conventional science no longer can bridge the elements arriving from the higher dimensions. This has left a void in understanding that has contributed to many of the misunderstandings in the scientific community.

With the advent of co-creative science, the mechanisms are in place to help humanity begin the long process to re-educate the human mind. Given that we are introducing a program that houses the components of co-creation and addresses the environment, we have a remarkable opportunity to advance an agenda that supports the transition from conventional science to co-creative science. What is more, we have in this model an opportunity to reorient science to include co-creative science as a viable and necessary way to move forward. Therefore, the Awakened Earth model serves to remind us that nature can be directly partnered with to advance a co-creative dynamic that ultimately serves all of life. With co-creative science comes an opportunity, not only to expand the consciousness, but to increase awareness in a means other than conventional science to address issues currently surfacing worldwide.

Laid out before you is a straightforward course that will become the foundation for the earth to be brought into balance. We have developed a series of processes that, when employed with care, will deliver harmony and balance to many diverse environmental challenges. The means to implement these processes is co-creative science.

Nature as a Cooperative Force

Nature has become a much-maligned influence in today's world. The force of nature is contrary to much of the world's understanding. Nature is, in its essence, a living force for intelligent balance. Nature has the inherent ability to come into balance, provided that humanity can change its view of nature.

Nature is an adjunct to humanity in that it responds to the influence brought about by human endeavors. Take, for example, the rainforests of Brazil: human domination has brought about changes in the biosphere that have altered life in the rainforest. Human consumption has weakened the balance of nature to such an extent that it is doubtful the rainforests will ever recover. Yet humanity seeks to capitalize on its resources, thereby further damaging the infrastructure to the entire continent of South America.

Until humanity accepts its role in the permanent destruction of these forests, there will be no rehabilitation. In other words, humanity must come to terms with its own contribution to a deteriorating ecosystem as the result of its thirst for development. Recognition of this fact is the beginning of hope for the generations that follow.

In western science, there has been a reluctance to broaden the scope of awareness. There has been an attempt to maintain the status quo by adhering to principles that are no longer appropriate. As we engage with the Awakened Earth co-creative model, we are breaking the mold and inviting the reader to think beyond the current scientific model.

Co-creative science is a relatively new phenomenon. It has its roots in the Perelandra Nature Center, where Machaelle Small Wright tapped into the benevolence and intelligence of the body of nature. She has devoted herself to the discipline of co-creative science while bringing forward scientific proof that nature can and will respond to human requests for help. She has learned to bring together factions of the unseen in order to fulfill a designated purpose.

Building on this knowledge, we came to the conclusion that nature was a willing participant in order to maximize quality of life for all life. Knowing this became our foundation, as we set forth with the Awakened Earth. As we devoted ourselves to the development of processes adequate for the challenges in the current environment, we realized the scope of the challenge we were undertaking.

The Awakened Earth flows from a place of purity and is constructed in such a way as to harness the power of co-creation while adhering to principles that underlie the natural order. Co-creation is a format for changing the way we view nature and presenting a viable alternative to conventional science. This work builds upon Machaelle Small Wright's findings and delivers it to humanity with the intent that environments, and thus all life, can be served using the co-creative model.

The Communication Factor

As this model was in development, we concluded that, in order to be successful, we had to bridge the language barrier in a way that was productive. While we were considering our options, we inadvertently stumbled upon making the pendulum work for us in additional ways. By expanding the number of responses, using additional movements with the pendulum, we gained a means of clarifying and enriching our "conversations." We embellished these movements with additional meaning. Having a willing partner, we imbued the new movements with the additional meanings. The result is the format we use today.

Our expanded pendulum responses diverge from the Perelandra model. Our communication link is more refined; therefore, we are able to converse across the dimensions with more effectiveness than a yes/no format provides. To those of you familiar with the Perelandra approach, we ask that you set it aside in favor of this more developed communication tool. You will find it more relevant as you become more familiar with the Awakened Earth model.

In terms of ease, the pendulum provides a visual dynamic that is useful. It allows us to clarify and expand our thinking in order to communicate more effectively. As you ask your questions, we can respond in more depth and accuracy by using the additional responses of this expanded format. As you become more skilled in using a pendulum, you will learn to recognize our ability to differentiate between "yes," "no," "possibly," "not quite accurate," "we don't know," or "ask more questions." We often will rely on the response "not quite accurate" to alert you to step away from a fixed response in favor of another possibility.

Given that we are bringing a brand new methodology forward, there will be times when communication efforts are an important factor in the fulfillment of an individual project. A project is, by definition, an environment receiving the benefit of the Awakened Earth energies. Communication is the key to a successful partnership as we address these environments because it brings together the elements required to fulfill an intention.

We anticipate some resistance to the communication factor. It will be worthwhile for each partnership to invest the time needed to perfect the communication issue. When we have established communication between the seen and the unseen, we will have surmounted the greatest obstacle to success. We have concluded that this method is sound, workable, and will produce results.

In order to establish a fully functioning partnership, the Awakened Earth Masters must first be invited. Nature will join the partnership once the intention is set. At this point, we come into alignment with your energy field. This sets the stage for us to bridge the distance between our understanding and yours. In addition, we bring to the partnership all the components needed to activate the dynamic of co-creation. Once this partnership is formed, we will supply the means to provide a balanced working environment.

Nature Is a Dynamic of Balance

Nature is a consciousness of balance. It follows that whenever nature is joined with humanity in a co-creative partnership, there is balance. It is as simple as that. Nature has, contained within its consciousness, energetic quotients for constructing all forms of balance. When humanity engages nature, nature brings to the partnership all that is needed to construct balance. Therefore, whenever humanity partners with nature, balance is assured. Think of nature as a benevolent friend who is eager to assist you.

To initiate a co-creative partnership, the human member brings an intention to nature. (Detailed instructions on the use of intention will follow in Chapter Five.) Once the intention is stated, nature coalesces around the intention and brings together the members necessary to fulfill the intention. For example, if you wish to supply an environment with a measure of stability so the environment can be brought to health, you would provide a request to allow the environment to come into balance. This would alert the general body of nature, and nature would bring together the suitable members to bring balance to the identified environment.

With the advent of co-creation, nature has a vehicle to engage humanity to expand the consciousness and bridge the unseen with the seen in a productive manner. This is the vehicle we have been waiting for. It gives us a conduit for communicating with humanity. With the addition of the expanded pendulum responses, we now have suitable means for engaging with humanity in a productive manner. Using the Awakened Earth model, we can further bridge the communication barrier and present a unified approach to deliver balance into countless environments around the globe.

Co-creation is the next arena of science to be incorporated into the grid of human consciousness. It will open frontiers that have never been contemplated.

Nature Offers a Dynamic of Change

As we have said, the Awakened Earth project functions in a new way. Rather than identifying beforehand the members who will be assisting you, the intention now serves to form the team, or co-creative partnership. While this is similar to other forms of co-creation, the Awakened Earth model broadens the scope of co-creation by stating an intention. The intention serves to initiate the co-creative partnership, which comes together to fulfill the intention. Humanity brings the intention to the table and nature fulfills it.

The Awakened Earth partnership is constructed in a manner that is substantively different from other formulas. The Awakened Earth Masters are the holders of the vision, given to them by the human partner, while nature is the implementer. The partnership is anchored by a framework designed to elevate the human consciousness while, at the same time, bringing balance and health to environments.

Extraordinary Means for Extraordinary Measures

In cooperation with the advanced measures we are presenting in *The Awakened Earth*, we also are aligning you with a consciousness of extraordinary means. This consciousness is, by and large, a stream of thought that has the ability to elevate all who come in contact with it. Let us try to explain.

Coming into partnership with the co-creative model we are introducing gives you an opportunity to function in accordance with a higher consciousness. In other words, each participant in the Awakened Earth project will be aligned with the most current information available to the totality of the consciousness. While some of you already engage the unseen in a variety of ways, we are asking that, whenever you participate in the Awakened Earth project, you utilize the methods we are outlining here. Incorporating these methods will ensure that each partnership is aligned with the co-creative principles presented in the Awakened Earth. We are certain you will find these methods far surpass any you have experienced before in any other co-creative formulas. These methods have been tested and are sound.

Each process contains within it elements that are compatible with the other processes; they will accumulate as you work with them on any given environment. As an environment receives an influx of energy from a process, it will begin to incorporate the elements present in the process. As you continue to work with the other processes, each environment will receive the benefit from earlier energy infusions, bringing into each environment a more sophisticated resonance even as the energy transforms the environment and gives it health.

What we are saying here is that each process is designed to work with other Awakened Earth processes. Their combined effect is exponential. Given that we are advancing a cutting-edge philosophy, we want you to appreciate the effectiveness of the combination of multiple Awakened Earth processes. We are sure you will find the results beyond imagining.

Within the Awakened Earth model is the means to deliver significant change to any environment receiving the benefit of the Awakened Earth energies. There also will be an instantaneous improvement of all aspects of the environment. Once the Awakened Earth has been acknowledged as an extraordinary means to bring balance to the earth, it is our belief that the earth will come into alignment far more quickly than imagined. We say this because we continue to see remarkable results where the Awakened Earth energies have been introduced into environments and ecosystems.

The Power of Love

Humanity is at a crossroads in its evolution. As we move into an era of self-responsibility, we remind you that you are engaging a consciousness much like your own. In nature, there is one constant: love. Love is the current that runs through all life and informs all living matter.

Nature holds the blueprint for everything that has form. Nature also informs all that is without form—with love. Love is the energy that runs through nature and gives meaning to all life. To engage nature is to engage love. Therefore, whenever the Awakened Earth is engaged, love is present, too.

Love binds together the invisible with the visible. Love is the power that heals and brings balance to imbalance. When love is present, there is balance. The two are inseparable. Love cannot exist without balance. Moreover, when love is present, there is nothing that cannot be healed. Because love is the constant, when you engage nature you are engaging love. When the heart is engaged, love is the active force, utilized by nature, to bring balance.

As you participate in the Awakened Earth project, you will be actively engaging your heart in your pursuit of balance. We are confident that once you have tasted the soothing nature of these processes, there will be no doubt that you have been touched by love. Love brings environments back to health. It is also the only resource that is pure. Love has no agenda other than to extend itself. Love has no equal.

Over time, I have found that nature is a constant and available resource. Nature will work with you in a manner that is compatible with your understanding. Once you have established a partnership, nature will bring together the unseen members necessary to fulfill your stated intention. It is not necessary for you to identify the individual unseen members. Nature will do that. Always know that the Awakened Earth Masters are a part of every partnership. There will be occasions for additional support from the unseen. You do not have to consider this need. That is one of the advantages of working in the Awakened Earth co-creative format. Nature and the AE Masters will do that for you. This ingenuity by nature is one of the most gratifying aspects of working co-creatively. You don't "have to know" who to invite into the partnership. Nor do you have to know how the universe operates. Nature knows. All you have to do is ask.

I often begin my questions to nature with "Do you know how to bring together a partnership for balance in my yard?" Or, "Do you know if we can effect change to the ecosystem in the Belgium Congo?" Usually the answer is "yes." Nature has the capacity to answer my questions as long as I give them a specific request. As an example, when I have a dilemma regarding an environment, I ask nature, "Is it possible to bring balance to the aphid population in the Great Smokies?" Nature will respond by telling me to augment my request to include the entire state of Tennessee. The expanded pendulum format allows me to communicate more fully and gives me the ability to understand what nature is suggesting. In this case, a larger environment was preferable to nature. I verify this by asking, "Is the state of Tennessee the environment you wish to work with for the aphids?" Nature replies, "Yes." Now I know we will be applying the Awakened Earth processes to the larger environment on behalf of the aphids. Nature knows this is in alignment with the higher order.

Note: To help sustain my energy during a session, I fuel myself with energy-building protein. Sessions usually last from twenty to thirty minutes.

Our capacity to hear you is a given. Nature can and will partner with you. Nature has the capacity to work with you and perform many tasks with you. What is more, there will be direct contact with the consciousness of nature, which is waiting and willing to co-create with you. In the past, there have been situations wherein the unseen had to relinquish its desire to partner directly with humanity because the unseen could not bridge the communication gap. With the advent of this model, we now have an advantage not present before.

CHAPTER 4

Balance Is a
Prerequisite for Health

As we discover that we are one with nature, we will also come to know a more balanced way to approach life. Coming to nature will mean coming to a balanced force of which we are all a part. This will give us a new working framework. Once the Awakened Earth model is recognized as a viable means to bring balance to numerous situations currently in need of assistance, I suspect there will be an outpouring of interest in this co-creative model. Nature has and will continue to help us mortals as we move ahead in our understanding of an interconnected earth.

Once we have a broader understanding of the capacity of nature to right our wrongs, we have the potential to bring balance to significant portions of the earth. Given that we are on the cusp of a new paradigm, we have an opportunity to alter the landscape while, at the same time, insuring a higher order. Over time, I have come to the point of allowing nature to direct many aspects of my life. This model can be used in many diverse situations, including business ventures, agricultural endeavors, personal situations, or any number of other life experiences.

Nature and Balance Are One

As we have said, nature is a consciousness of balance. Therefore, when nature is engaged, balance is assured. The momentum of the Awakened Earth is derived from balance. Nature is participating in this co-creative endeavor. Therefore, whatever comes forth from the co-creative endeavor will be balanced. It is the law.

Balance brings health and provides an environment with the necessary elements to maintain health. Balance has at its core the components necessary to allow an environment to come into a state of harmony. Harmony is an adjunct to balance. As an environment gains harmony, it will also become more balanced. Together, balance and harmony help an environment come into health, bringing stability, which is at the core of a healthy environment. The role of nature is to ensure balance, which leads to health, which leads to stability. These are the building blocks of a healthy environment. Without these building blocks, there can be no foundation for stability.

Balance is the inherent quality in nature. Nature brings balance to any situation in need of balance because nature operates *only* from a state of balance. Balance is the state of being required for an environment to become strengthened. Balance is incorporated by engaging nature in every co-creative partnership; engaging a co-creative partnership will automatically establish a framework for balance. Balance has within it the corresponding elements required for any environment to be elevated into a state of balance. Setting an intention also calls upon additional factors that can deliver balance.

A state of balance is the condition necessary for any environment to be considered healthy. By stating an intention to the partnership, further balance is introduced into the framework of the partnership. Bringing an intention to the partnership sets into motion irrefutable laws that govern all aspects of the Awakened Earth project. The stated intention establishes a working environment that becomes aligned with the natural laws present in all of the natural order.

As this work will demonstrate, the environment called into existence is in balance with the operating forces in the universe. The fact that balance is incorporated into the formation of each partnership guarantees that all work that proceeds from each partnership also will be in balance. It can be no other way.

Coming to nature assures that an environment will have the building blocks to maintain health, provided that the environment is given the necessary elements through the Awakened Earth energies. These energies are consistent with balance and have the capacity to bring stability and even health. Each environment, while connected to the whole, is an entity unto itself. As we address the circumstances of an individual environment, we are also addressing the whole.

As we introduce these co-creative principles to the ordinary human mind, we are cognizant that many will discover the power of these remarkable principles. The principles of co-creation are relatively new and are not widely known. Co-creation, working in partnership with unseen counterparts, is a relatively new phenomenon. We are confident that, once these co-creative principles are experienced, there will be a broader understanding.

Nature Is a Balanced Consciousness

Coming to nature is like coming to an inspired source for answers to perplexing problems. Nature has the ingredients to harness universal well-being while, at the same time, presiding over a more consistent body of truth. While this is new philosophy, it is consistent with universal law. Moreover, as these doctrines of co-creation are made available to humanity, they will become recognized as the highest level of science known to man. Once some of the results of the Awakened Earth processes are known, it is likely many will come to this work seeking solutions to perplexing problems. As this work is given a chance, there will be more opportunities for humanity to utilize these principles in many situations.

This project is an example of the best of co-creation. It has no agenda other than to serve the higher good. It promises to favor no one and to benefit all. As we move into the new millennium, there will be ample opportunity to exercise co-creation. This phenomenon has the potential to reverse eons of adverse conditions. It offers substantive solutions.

While co-creation has advanced, it is still in its infancy. Many of its attributes have begun to be recognized. It has taken Europe to new levels of advancement in farming and is producing significant results throughout the entire European continent. Moreover, the results are gaining wider recognition. There are applications underway to improve many facets of farming that are co-creative in origin. As word of this phenomenon spreads, there have been significant numbers of the European population investing in co-creative science.

In the beginning of the co-creative movement, Europe became the guiding force. It began in Scotland with Findhorn. As this program took root in consciousness, another co-creative endeavor was spawned in the United States. In the 1970s, Machaelle Small Wright founded Perelandra, a Nature Research Center outside of Washington, DC, for the purpose of exploring co-creation with nature. She has delivered a program of remarkable consistency that exercises co-creation. Through her research, she has introduced the co-creative philosophy into the mainstream. In an attempt to improve the quantity and quality of gardens, she has developed some of the most innovative programs, which have altered the gardening landscape.

Wright also applied the co-creative principles to establish new methods of health care. While her focus has been primarily in the arena of human health care, the Awakened Earth project is focused on the environment. By bringing co-creation to the environment, we have broadened the model so that we can bring balance and health to large portions of earth.

The Awakened Earth is an attempt to stabilize the entire planet. This large-scale pursuit has never been attempted before. This model's potential for success lies in equipping humanity with the knowledge to implement the processes effectively. Furthermore, we are committed to bringing this project into a workable format in order to establish co-creation as an effective methodology. The Awakened Earth model has vital new components that are relevant to bringing balance into environments throughout the world. Each environment will come into balance based upon its individual need.

Contained in this book are some of the most advanced methods ever presented. With this knowledge comes the responsibility to implement each process with care. Never before has such a large-scale program on behalf of the environment been attempted. It is an unprecedented opportunity to help all living matter. As nature comes to this work, it assures humanity of a project with balance. Balance is the common denominator throughout the Awakened Earth.

Given that we are entering an age of unprecedented change, the Awakened Earth will bring to humanity the ability to reverse damage to large regions of the earth. As this begins to happen, conditions will begin to strengthen, and balance will emerge in a new way. Furthermore, this project will help humanity to view itself differently. Humanity thinks of itself as separate from the natural world; actually, humanity is an integral part of the overall natural order. There is the perception of separation on the part of humanity. As humanity comes to terms with its common roots with the natural order, and hence with nature itself, humanity will begin to realize its scope of influence.

Humanity has begun to challenge its impact on the natural world. The next step is the full realization of its connection with all living matter. We have ordained this model of co-creation as the most suitable model to allow the earth to come into a more balanced state.

As I have said before, many of the developments regarding the Awakened Earth have transpired over time. When this project was first conceived, I had no idea the direction it would eventually take. Nevertheless, as time went on, it became apparent to me that something remarkable was taking place. Many environments receiving the benefit of the Awakened Earth methods were responding in a way that was new. California, in particular, was coming into a more balanced state, as evidenced by the increase in the water tables, especially in the year 2006. Once these processes were initiated, the reservoirs began to fill. Nature assured me that this development was directly linked to the introduction of the Awakened Earth energies. Nature also said that once the entire environment was treated with these processes, there would be a gradual increase in the amount of light. This is exactly what has happened.

Light, in my understanding, is the quotient of consciousness residing in an environment at the time of implementation of the Awakened Earth processes. In other words, the amount of light will change depending upon two things: first, the consciousness impacts the environment and second, the insertion of the Awakened Earth energies impacts the environment. Take for example, western North Carolina, as the broader ecosystem was given help to restore the water tables, the greater environment increased its amount of light.

Coming to Nature for Help

In the coming years, there is likely to be a reason for nature and humanity to come together in co-creation to establish a balanced earth. It is also likely that this coming together will help bring a more balanced consciousness. What we have in the Awakened Earth project is a program of co-creation that has the capacity to balance the earth and the consciousness. As this happens, there will be a more sophisticated energy coming in to lift the consciousness and give humanity the ability to achieve greater harmony and, therefore, health. Nature and humanity, when joined in co-creation, have the ability to solve what seems to be unsolvable.

Nature and humanity are part of the greater consciousness. As they join in forming co-creative partnerships, they will have the capacity to bring solutions to the world's stage. We, of nature and beyond, are waiting for humanity to recognize the full capacity of co-creative partnerships. These partnerships can reverse decades of damage to global environments and return habitats to their natural state.

Many environments are already coming into balance. In addition, there have been other environments that have begun the long process of returning to health. The examples of improving environments are mounting. In the southeastern United States, there have been numerous occasions to deliver balance. As this balance has been delivered, Lake Lanier, northeast of Atlanta, has filled. Other aquifers and reservoirs have reached high levels.

Moreover, the hurricanes that developed in 2009 behaved in a manner that demonstrated the effectiveness of the Awakened Earth energies to subdue these storms and direct their paths away from the mainland. These storms, and the waters over which they traveled, received the benefit of the Awakened Earth energies. The storms did not cause loss or damage. The savings in dollars is immense.

Environments Are in Jeopardy

Given that we are in pursuit of balance throughout the natural world, let us identify some environments that have sustained great harm. These environments are capable of bringing balance to the Earth, provided that they receive the energies available through the Awakened Earth model. These environments have the capacity to restructure large segments of the natural world. They also have the added benefit of demonstrating to the world the power of co-creation. Co-creation will demonstrate how the earth can regain its balance through applied cooperative action, using the Awakened Earth model. The environments are as follows:

- The mountains of Ecuador and Peru

- The Himalayan Mountains in Tibet

- The Ganges River in India

- The Sahara Desert in Africa

As these environments are treated with the energies available through the Awakened Earth project, they will begin to come into balance in a manner necessary for the entire planet to gain stability. As we move into and rebalance these environments, there will be a reconfiguring of all of the adjoining environments. This will offer the earth even more balance than she needs.

In an effort to augment the natural order, as these particular environments become stabilized, the earth will harness the power derived from the Awakened Earth practices to become more balanced. Each of these endeavors has the potential to produce significant results. Each will open the doorway for future co-creative endeavors in these regions. Once the power of this project to deliver results is recognized, there are certain to be many who will want to advance the cause of co-creation. Generally speaking, co-creation surpasses any other delivery system currently in existence.

CHAPTER 5

The Awakened Earth Formula for Forming Partnerships

As the world rapidly changes, there is a need for new solutions. These solutions have their roots in a larger universe. By its nature, humanity is an expanding organism. To match the requirements of humanity's expansion, a program now exists to address the emerging needs of humanity at a crossroad. These times call for a restructuring of many major systems, including several deteriorating environments.

This chapter paves the way to the Awakened Earth model of co-creation. It gives you all that you need to establish a working relationship with your partners in nature. What follows in the remainder of this Awakened Earth presentation will not only identify the emerging needs, but provide the means to do so.

Creating a Partnership

As we undertake the creation of a more advanced formula for co-creative partnerships, we set in motion an entirely new model for working with the unseen. This model has been introduced by the Awakened Earth Masters for the purpose of fulfilling the Awakened Earth model of co-creation.

Before we go any further, let us introduce ourselves. We are: Metatron, Archangel Michael, St. Germain, and the Planetary Logos, whose job is to oversee the Earth in this time of great change. With this undertaking, we have consented to an unprecedented commitment to help the earth and advance the balance of nature.

The Awakened Earth is unprecedented. No other formula exists today to bring health and balance to environments across the globe. In other words, this remarkable work gives you the opportunity to work in partnership with Masters who have the expertise to deliver to you a product that is not only workable, but profound.

A partnership begins with a desire to help an environment reach a greater level of stability. To identify an environment in need of help requires the establishment of a co-creative partnership. The partnership is the foundation of all Awakened Earth activities. For our purposes, an environmental project is any request brought to nature for the purpose of bringing an environment into a higher order, so that its health and balance are maximized.

To initiate a partnership, the human partner must say, "I wish to enter into a co-creative partnership with the Awakened Earth Masters." With this simple statement, a partnership is born.

The Power of Intention

Next, you will need to provide an intention. The Masters will coalesce when you state your intention. The intention sets the foundation for the partnership. Nature will automatically bring together the individual members needed to fulfill the intention. As the partnership comes together to support the intention, there will be an added measure of balance in the partnership, because balance automatically occurs whenever nature is called into a co-creative partnership.

Nature will provide the means for any co-creative endeavor to fulfill its intention. The dynamic of co-creation is the result of nature and a human partner joining forces to fulfill an intention. What follows is the co-creative dynamic in action.

An intention holds the blueprint for the co-creative partnership. You could say the intention is the arrow you have launched into a universe waiting to fulfill it. Whenever nature and humanity come together for the purpose of fulfilling an intention, a co-creative partnership is formed.

Intentions are, by nature, vehicles to co-create in compliance with the natural order. They have a unique function and serve as the doorway to all operating co-creative partnerships. To function in partnership with nature is the most reliable means for sustaining balance. Nature has the dynamic of balance within its consciousness. Therefore, whenever nature is called upon, there is balance.

To form an intention is one of the most important functions in the creation of a co-creative partnership. It gives form to the partnership. For example, when an intention is presented to nature, nature rearranges itself to bind together the necessary elements to fulfill the intention. It is not necessary to understand how this works. It is much like switching on a light switch; it is not necessary to understand how the light comes to you.

Allow nature to be part of the mystery. Mental understanding is unnecessary.

As we move into greater understanding of co-creation, we will be educating you in the foundational qualities of working in a partnership with nature. Nature is fluent in form and function. Nature also has the ability to come together with humanity in order to perform certain tasks that benefit the entire natural order. Because we are introducing a model of co-creation that is in harmony with nature, there can be no doubt of its ability to fulfill a balanced intention.

Let us take the time to educate you in the best way to approach an intention. We are experts in forming and fulfilling intentions. Furthermore, we have influence in establishing correct language for an intention. What do we mean by this? Bring your intention to your partnership. We will work with you in establishing the best language for your intention. Let's say your intention states:

"I want to bring balance to the mountains that are experiencing an infestation of beetles."

We would work with you, using the pendulum, to amend this intention so that it complies with the natural order. With your pendulum, this can easily be done. The reworked intention would read:

"To bring balance to the pine bark beetle in the Appalachian Mountains."

Now we have a specific species in a specific area, which complies with the natural order.

Another example might be: "I want to reverse the damage to the trees in my neighborhood."

We would change this to read, "Bring harmony to the area west of Interstate 77 and extending to the Tennessee border, so that the woodlands can maintain optimum balance."

Do you see the difference? The restated intention has a specific boundary and is addressing a specific environment, the woodlands west of Interstate 77, extending to the Tennessee line. Now nature is in a position to fulfill your intention.

With the help of your partners, an intention can be restated to comply with the natural order. This will alleviate confusion and initiate a co-creative partnership that is in alignment. Nature can then fulfill your intention with ease. We suggest you practice forming an intention before launching your co-creative partnership. This will help you become familiar with the process of stating specific intentions.

The Art of Asking Questions

The next key element to any successful co-creative partnership is to form clear and concise questions. It is remarkable the difference good questions can make. Because we are developing the art of communication between your unseen partners and you, it stands to reason that we must have a clear understanding of each other. In other words, we must be able to communicate with you much as you communicate with each other. We cannot overemphasize the importance of stating a question with clarity. It is the single most important skill you must learn.

To give you an example: if a question is stated in a way that elicits a "yes" or "no" response, we can answer you clearly. Such a question could be: "Is there a need for this environment to be treated?" To this, the response can easily be "yes" or "no." In the early stages of your partnership, we will work with you using a "yes" and "no" format. If the question is: "Can this environment become balanced and brought into harmony?" we could not give a "yes" or "no" response. This question is asking two things; therefore, we could not give you a clear response. A question needs to be stated in a way that requests a "yes" or "no" response. It may help to write the question down to clarify it for yourself before presenting it to your unseen partners.

Examples of poor questions: "Can I balance and harmonize the area adjacent to my back yard? Is it possible to strengthen and balance the reservoir in town? Would you be able to bring balance to the woodlands in the next township? Can I deliver the right amount of help to the forests in my state?" All of these questions are unfit to answer. Each one is without specific identification and is vague in terms of what is being requested.

To improve these questions and allow them to be suitable for us to answer, they would need to be improved as follows: Can I help bring balance to the woodlands behind my house? Is it possible to balance the reservoir in Loma Linda, CA.? Would you be able to bring balance to the vacant land on Route 40 in Hackensack, NJ? Can I deliver balance to the state forest in Bellingham, WA?

As you break a question down, remember that you are looking for a "yes" or "no" response. As you practice asking questions, this will become easier. While we are urging a "yes" or "no" response in the formation of questions, we also remind you to become proficient in using the pendulum. Utilizing the expanded pendulum responses, we can usually come to a place of common understanding. For example, when you ask: "Can the woodlands behind my house be treated using the Awakened Earth processes?" we may respond with "possibly." In that case, you would be alerted to ask a second question: "Are the woodlands behind my house suitable for the Awakened Earth methods?" In this case, we would give you a "yes" or "no" response, because of our clearer understanding of your question.

We want you to realize that we can hear you, so it may help to speak your questions out loud. We are skilled in ascertaining meaning from the human perspective. However, it also is important for you to be aware of the context of your question. Give yourself time to become clear so that your question is clear. Again, we urge you to practice.

We are introducing to you a formula for working with the unseen, which has far-reaching implications. This work will bring an awareness that changes the way nature is understood. Through the formation of a co-creative partnership, nature will inform humanity with its wisdom. Once nature has entered into partnership with humanity, it can bring its knowledge to any situation needing help. What is more, nature has the expertise to identify specific pockets of imbalance and give the measures to correct them.

The art of asking questions is paramount to working effectively with the unseen, to ensure that communication is readily understood by both parties. To enhance this communication, questions must be asked in a way that elicits a response that is clear to both parties. This includes the ability to formulate clear and direct questions without assuming an answer beforehand. Most of the time, communication can be clarified using the pendulum and the expanded responses it provides.

Now that we have an expanded response format, we urge you to utilize it. With this expanded format, we are in a better position to have a conversation with you. For example, as you are determining an environment using the Awakened Earth model, we want to be able to discern with clarity the exact environment you are considering. When we have established the correct perimeters of the environment you are addressing, using the expanded format, we have a much greater opportunity for meeting success. As you embark upon using this new format, we ask you to keep in mind that we are attempting to give you workable solutions for an entirely new era.

As you become familiar with forming an intention, you will begin to develop a sense for appropriate language. For example, when I begin to write an intention, I start with a general statement of intent. Then I ask my partnership to bring my intention statement into the fullest expression. I do this by listening and intuiting with my unseen partners. With the pendulum, I ascertain the vernacular that best suits my intention. Nature will work with you in a manner that is compatible with your understanding.

Nature has the capacity to work with you and perform many tasks with you. There will be direct contact with the consciousness of nature, which is waiting and willing to co-create with you. In the past, there have been situations wherein the unseen had to relinquish its desire to partner directly with humanity because the unseen could not bridge the communication gap. With the advent of this model, we now have an advantage not present before.

Opening and Closing a Session with Nature

When you begin a session with nature, you have an opportunity to work in partnership with a consciousness capable of bringing balance into an environment of your choosing. The steps outlined below will guide you. The steps offer substantive guidelines to help you formulate how to work with your partners in nature.

1. Begin by centering within your own being. For our purposes, we will refer to your center as the heart. Spend a few moments bringing yourself into alignment with the greater you.

2. State the intention. The intention alerts the greater body of nature that along with the Awakened Earth Masters, will assist you in fulfilling the stated intention. To determine an intention is primary in setting the direction for the partnership. The intention serves as the blueprint for the co-creative partnership. It is important that the intention complies with the natural order. Intentions are to be specific so that the unseen will know the precise environment you are working with. The Masters have the ability to bring together the exact members to fulfill any stated intention. It is important that the intention complies with the natural order. For example, when you state that you wish to bring rainfall into a particular environment, we will align ourselves to that particular environment so that the fulfillment of the intention will be in accord with the natural order. Intentions are to be specific so that the unseen will know the precise environment you are working with. The precise location of the environment is necessary so that your partners can fulfill your intention.

3. Take out The Awakened Earth Processes Checklist. Using your pendulum, identify, with your partners, which of

the processes are needed to address the stated intention. Usually the processes are implemented in numeric order.

4. Determine the amount of light present by asking your partnership. Note it on your Project Worksheet. The light quotient will be necessary for use with some of the processes, but not all of them.

5. Implement the processes, in numeric order, with your partners. Verify that they have been completed.

6. Again using your pendulum, check with your partners for follow-up information. If a follow-up session is indicated, note the follow-up session date on your worksheet. *(I have found that noting the follow-up sessions on a calendar helps me to keep track of environmental sessions and follow-ups.)*

7. To close the session, simply say to your partners, "Thank you, we close for now in the honor of oneness." Wait ten to fifteen seconds for the session to fully close.

Sample Environmental Project Worksheet

Date: July 20, 2009

Session: #1

Follow-up date: July 27, 2009

Project: WNC Moisture Balance   *Light:* 6

Description of Environment: The counties west of Interstate 77, south to the South Carolina border and west to the Tennessee border.

Intention: To bring balance to the WNC mountains so that rainfall will be in harmony with the natural order.

Co-Creative Partners Present: The Awakened Earth Masters

Processes called for: # 12 Frequency Stabilization for 60 seconds

Expanded Pendulum Responses

The advent of the following expanded pendulum responses allows me to communicate more effectively with my team. These responses alleviate much misunderstanding when communicating with the unseen. With the pendulum, the Awakened Earth Masters give me the answers to my questions. In this way, I can pin down a more specific response, which allows us to move into greater understanding and eliminates some of the guesswork. Furthermore, I have developed the habit of asking them, "Have I understood you correctly?" I also have learned to utilize other questions such as: "Is this what you meant?" "Is this complete?" "Do you understand what I mean?" With the addition of these questions, I have become quite proficient in bringing the material forward.

The expanded pendulum responses have allowed us to interface with you, our human partners, with more understanding and efficiency. Once these Awakened Earth processes are in the hands of those desiring to work with them, there is every likelihood that some of you reading this material will be ready to begin your own co-creative endeavor. When you participate in the Awakened Earth project, you will be contributing to the overall balance of many of earth's deteriorating environments. In other words, this project is capable of lifting an environment into a quality of existence never before known.

With the advent of the expanded pendulum responses, there is opportunity to work in a co-creative partnership using the latest "technologies." This should curtail any possible misunderstandings as you move into this work. The Awakened Earth processes, and the energy they contain, are the latest mechanisms for implementing co-creative endeavors. As such, the processes will deliver energetic infusions capable of bringing an environment into balance.

Together, we will identify the suitable processes we will implement with you, giving you assurance that we understand each other. As you become proficient with your pendulum, our communication ability will increase. Therefore, we ask you to rely on your pendulum and not your intuition. In the event that your pendulum counters your intuition, we ask that you verify what your intuition may be suggesting. In this way, we can direct you more clearly. The pendulum offers a visual aid that gives you a clear response.

It also is important for you to become comfortable with the co-creative format we are presenting and especially with the use of the expanded pendulum responses. We have determined that the best way to communicate is through the use of a pendulum.

After you have opened a fully functioning co-creative partnership, we ask you to do the following: In front of you, hold your pendulum still and ask your partners to demonstrate the individual pendulum movements. Ask them to show you a "yes" response. Then ask them to show you a "no" response. Then ask to be shown a "possibly" response and so forth until you have been shown each of the six pendulum movements. You will find that nature knows each response and will demonstrate each one to you. It is important to hold your hand still while asking your partners to show you these responses. Remember, nature is prepared to help you. Since this is our main communication tool, it is best that you practice these movements until you are comfortable with them. Your partners are more than willing to teach you.

Following are the expanded pendulum responses:

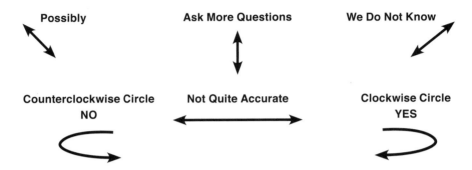

As these responses become familiar, we are certain our communication will flourish. With the expanded pendulum responses, the co-creative partnerships will begin to function effortlessly. Over time, we expect to develop a satisfactory means of communication. For example, as you learn to communicate effectively, we will be able to direct you with more accuracy.

Each partnership will have unique patterns of communication, which will evolve over time. This will ease the burden for both of us. As we gain comfort with each other, we will be in a position to educate you further using the established pendulum format. Furthermore, as we become accustomed to each other, the communication will become as easy as speaking in conversation. We have initiated a unique format for conversing with the unseen.

Criteria for Selecting Environments

As we come to the point in the Awakened Earth project where we need to select suitable environments, we wish to give you criteria for evaluating an environment. The criteria will address the suitability for an environment to receive the energies from the Awakened Earth processes. Furthermore, we will give you a compendium of information that will help you to make suitable selections. It is not necessary to be on location to implement the Awakened Earth processes. They can be done in the comfort of your own home. The quantum world allows us to impact any environment regardless of time or distance.

The process for choosing environments

1. Identify the property using specific boundaries. For example, appropriate designations of property might be: the woods in my county that border on Route 27 to the north and the river on the west. Once you have specifically identified the boundaries, your partners can evaluate the property with you.

2. Come into the stillness by placing your awareness in the heart. This will bring you into alignment with the unseen energies that are present to assist you. When you have established this connection, we will be in a position to advise you.

3. Give your partners time to evaluate the feasibility of your selected environment. This evaluation should take approximately thirty to sixty seconds.

4. Accept the decisions of your unseen spiritual partners, as they are in the best position to determine suitability.

Once these criteria have been met, you will be ready to form an intention. When the intention has been verified the next steps can be implemented. To guide you, refer to "Opening and Closing a Session with Nature."

The Awakened Earth Processes Checklist will then help you determine the steps you will need to take to fulfill your intention.

A form to use as the checklist appears in the Appendices at the end of this book.

Using an Environmental Project Worksheet, a copy of which also is provided in the Appendices, will give you a way to track each environment and also will provide you with a format that is easy to follow. The worksheets have been designed to help you keep track of the plans and progress on each environment. Use a separate worksheet for each environment. It is important to keep accurate records so that each environment will have the benefit of detailed information. Accurate record-keeping also will help the overall Awakened Earth movement by providing evidence of the process' effectiveness. Over time, these records will prove the validity of this magnificent work.

As long as we have a standard for evaluating the selection of environments, there will be a consistency in all of the Awakened Earth co-creative partnerships. These standards are to be followed with care.

Standards for evaluating the selection of environments

1. Release other formulas for co-creative partnerships you may have been working with.

2. Give your attention to the Awakened Earth partnership, understanding that it will call together the components necessary for your specific endeavor.

3. Give the partnership the ability to assess the validity of your particular endeavor. They will give you alignment with the natural order.

4. Grant your partnership the right to help you with your designated environment. They will give you a bona fide

co-creative endeavor simply by aligning themselves with your environment.

5. Be firm in your decision to use only this formula. Other co-creative formulas are not suitable for The Awakened Earth, as this model embraces a new philosophy designed to bring harmony throughout the natural world. The measures presented in the Awakened Earth are qualitatively different. It is important that they be used uniformly and consistently.

6. Understand that this project is like no other. It originates in an arena of thought beyond previous accessibility and has been conceived in an entirely new way. Avoid any tendency to judge this project in terms of or in comparison to other projects.

7. Come to your partnership with an open mind and heart, as well as a willingness to learn.

8. Bring your intention to the Awakened Earth Masters for viability of your project. Trust that they will work with you to find suitable language for your co-creative endeavor.

9. Allow the partnership the right to override you. If their decisions disagree with your intuitive decisions, give your unseen partners the opportunity to explain and clarify the position until you can understand it from their perspective.

10. Learn to recognize the value of working in an environment of pure light. While the experience may differ from anything you have done before, when you become accustomed to working with light, you may find that it changes your perspective in many areas.

Environmental Changes

As this project unfolds, there will be opportunities to bring healthy changes to many environments. The recent wildfires in California produced an opportunity for us to use the Awakened Earth processes. Our intention was to help burned land to rejuvenate in a manner that would help establish a unified ecosystem that was capable of coming into balance. The soil has begun to increase its vitality. In the event that we are able to bring you specific data supporting the balance that has been created in the fire zones, we will do so. Remember that this is a work in progress and, therefore, results will be slow in coming in the beginning. However, once the word is out and the Awakened Earth is recognized for its caliber and purity, we will publish details on the Awakened Earth website. Each of you can be on the lookout for local news, which gives credence to this co-creative endeavor.

It will be of value to those persons committing to this work to understand the general mechanisms that will be used to engage harmony and balance. Harmony and balance are the underpinnings of a healthy environment. To achieve this state of being is the purpose of the Awakened Earth.

To capitalize on the momentum already set in motion by the introduction of the Awakened Earth model, it is hoped that those of you reading this material will consider joining with the unseen to institute a program of significant change. Under the auspices of the Awakened Earth Masters lies an opportunity never before presented to humanity. We have given you a model that not only can reverse existing damage but that is prepared to elevate the consciousness and deliver to the earth much needed elements for balance and health. Also, never before have the Masters given consent to a co-creative endeavor. With the Awakened Earth, we are making an exception.

As we prepare to take you into the heart of The Awakened Earth concept, we want to clarify how these processes work together for the betterment of each environment. While it is understood by many, it bears stating that nature and the Awakened Earth Masters are responsible for the betterment of the properties treated by the Awakened Earth processes. Each process is imbued with specific elements and energies that have been formulated to allow each environment the encouragement it needs to function in a healthy manner. To begin with, each environment has differing needs and, therefore, will require the application of different processes in order to maximize its health. Each process has the ability to create a balanced state that allows the individual environment to flourish and regain health. Health is determined by how the environment responds to its challenges as it undergoes transformation to its more refined state. In order to be considered healthy, an environment will behave in ways which are in alignment with the natural order. The human mind wants measurements that cannot be given at this point in the Awakened Earth's development. While we know this is not satisfactory to some of you, we ask that you put aside your need to know in favor of trusting the outcomes of the many environments that have already been treated.

In order to function at the highest level, some environments will need several applications of the Awakened Earth processes. This will insure that the environment has the best chance to rejuvenate and come into balance. When the treatments are complete and nature has signed off on a particular environment, there are likely to be noticeable improvements. As western North Carolina was brought into balance, while addressing the severe drought, many were aware that the overall environment began to behave in a manner that was congruent with its health in earlier times.

The individual needs of each environment can be addressed by the intention brought to it by the Awakened Earth practitioner. In other words, the environment can be brought into a healthier state by defining an intention and then bringing that intention to the Awakened Earth co-creative partnership. Once the intention has been established, the opportunity opens to engage in a co-creative partnership with the Awakened Earth Masters with the ultimate goal of improving the health and balance of an individual environment.

The Earth Is at a Crossroad

While we have addressed the environment as a whole, we have not discussed why you should get involved. The earth needs you. The times are calling for help from humanity. Nature and the Masters have come together precisely at this time in evolution so that humanity will have the tools to take back stewardship of the earth. The earth has lingered at the edge of her ability to remain stable for far too long.

What can you, the reader, do to get involved? Join the Awakened Earth movement. Be a representative who chooses to make a difference.

Earth Is a Receptacle of Balance

As we promote well-being for the earth, we are mindful of the aims of *The Awakened Earth*. It is likely that some of you will engage in partnerships in order to stabilize environments that are near and dear to you. Perhaps some of you will want to step out further and consider embracing global environments that are in need of humanity's help. As we launch this program, giving you the tools to harness nature's power along with the Awakened Earth Master's power, we are setting the stage for the earth to be the recipient of the balance she needs to live cooperatively with humanity. We are bringing you the pathway into fields of creation that can deliver significant balance to earth's body. As the balance accumulates, nature will oversee the dispersing of the new energies so that the earth will receive only the energies that are considered to be in alignment with the higher order. This is not something you need to be concerned about. We will handle the balance of the incoming energies. We are hopeful that this material will resonate with sufficient numbers of you to help the earth in the time of her greatest need. As we shift the balance of nature into numerous environments, there will be improvements immediately.

Nature has been waiting for the time when humanity was able to assume direct contact with its intelligence so that the larger issues of global imbalance could be addressed. That time has come. We are standing by. We welcome you into the family of co-creation where you will find solutions to issues you never dreamed were possible.

Nature's View of Global Warming

There has been a school of thought that disputes the validity of global warming. From our perspective, global warming is a factor in some of earth's difficulties. For one thing, the frequent weather disturbances can be attributed to global warming. Major disturbances worldwide have occurred at an alarming rate. Global warming has its roots in excess carbon dioxide. Carbon dioxide is the byproduct of industrialization. Until recently, nature could assimilate the increase in carbon dioxide emissions. However, in the 1990s when the earth's population reached a tipping point, nature was no longer capable of maintaining balance worldwide.

The good news is that help for the earth is in your hands. The Awakened Earth provides the way. However, to remain in balance, the earth will need many helpers to apply the processes presented in this book. We, the Awakened Earth Masters, have been waiting for the time when humanity was ripe and ready to take up its mantle and help the earth come into balance. These times are upon us. We urge you to thoughtfully consider your participation in this magnificent endeavor. If you choose to help, an adventure awaits you as you give the earth and yourself a chance to be born anew.

The problems the earth is now facing may seem insurmountable, but we want you to know that we can and will solve them together. We have come forward at this time to initiate the Awakened Earth model, for it is time for co-creation to blossom and grow. The means are here. Will you join the effort and honor the earth?

In the not-too-distant future, there will be many opportunities to help the earth. What this means to you, the reader, is that you have the opportunity to participate in the most advanced and far-reaching endeavor ever presented to humanity. Will you form a co-creative partnership? Will you join the Awakened Earth movement? Will you be an advocate for life? These are the questions you need to ask yourself. We are ready to join you.

CHAPTER 6

The Heart of the
Awakened Earth

Evolutionary Measures for the New World

The Awakened Earth is a new and fresh approach to bringing health and balance to jeopardized environments throughout the world. The coordination of this co-creative effort to solve some of the more difficult challenges facing humanity has, itself, been a co-creative effort. Out of necessity, we have developed a format that is unlike any other.

The Awakened Earth was conceived when the author sought solutions for bringing balance to extreme weather conditions. These conditions had become unmanageable through more established means, and humanity was paying a high price. In hopes of finding a solution, this project was born.

The author first conceived of the idea to help environments come into balance by using co-creative means, but did not yet know the extent to which it could be valuable to the entire planet. Gradually we discovered together that, by initiating new energy, environments could be brought into balance. We soon learned that, once these processes were introduced into an environment, significant changes began to take place. The results were impressive and went beyond what we had thought possible.

Whenever these processes have been introduced, there has been measurable improvement in the overall balance of the specified environment. For example, in California, we have noticed that the land that had been burned in and around San Diego has begun to produce vegetation not seen in the ecosystem for nearly a century. What this means to us is that the help offered by the Awakened Earth processes is contributing directly to the growth of indigenous vegetation. With the return of indigenous plant life, the entire ecosystem has begun to recover its natural state of harmony and balance. As this continues, the southern California landscape will begin to recover in a way that is healthy. Over time, the entire ecosystem will become balanced and sustainable as long as there is a continuation of co-creative action to maintain this ecosystem.

We were witnessing the power of co-creation and new energies to deliver results to environments. Out of this discovery, we have developed a model that will deliver the needed properties into each selected environment. This, in turn, will bring the necessary elements into the environment to alleviate some of the imbalances causing distress. As these energies are introduced into an environment, they will begin to incorporate a new capacity for balance.

Shortly after the Awakened Earth processes were introduced into an environment, we began to see the impact the processes were having. For example, along the Florida coastline, we observed the conditions of the beaches improving. Beach erosion was lessened. The dune grasses became more abundant. The overall ecology of the ecosystem began to come into balance. This made us optimistic that once the Awakened Earth processes had been introduced into several environments, there would be significant change to the overall earth. As a result of these and other environmental changes, we gave the Awakened Earth project the support necessary to help begin the process of reclaiming environmental health for major portions of the earth. Because of the encouraging results of early trials of this model, we now believe the Awakened Earth model has the ability to heal the earth.

As I have worked with these processes, I have come to understand that an initial session with an environment usually consists of three or four of the following fifteen processes. An initial session usually can be completed within a forty-five-minute time frame. Subsequent sessions usually entail the implementation of two processes. However, once a project is underway, I have often found that there is only one process to be done. Rather than anticipate a lengthy time investment, these sessions are remarkably simple and short. When you gain a little experience, I am sure you will agree. As you become proficient in implementing the processes, I am confident you will come away with a sense of renewal as well as the inspiration to continue.

Because we are bringing you a new way to alleviate environmental imbalances, we want you to realize the significance of how the processes come together. Each process can be utilized alone or in conjunction with others. As we get into applying the processes, it is important to realize the continuity that has been established throughout all the processes. Some of the processes are utilized more than others. Some processes may never be called for, depending upon the needs of the individual environments selected for help. Gradually, as you work with the processes, you will discover a rhythm.

Given that the people on this planet are entering a new age of enlightenment, we are offering a new set of tools to bring balance and harmony to earth. The tools we have created are the most effective means for helping environments come into a state of balance.

One of the factors necessary to bring harmony to individual environments and to the entire planet is light. Earth is currently experiencing a period of adjustment, as a result of incorporating more light. Light is the dynamic force necessary for the earth to come into alignment with her counterparts in the galaxy.

To help you to visualize the implementation of the processes we have supplied the following illustrations for you. Each illustrates the use of the heart or the crown chakra to direct the Awakened Earth energies into a particular environment. While not all processes are represented the ones shown will supply you with adequate visualization for implementation.

Sample Illustrations of Some Processes and a Co-Creative Session

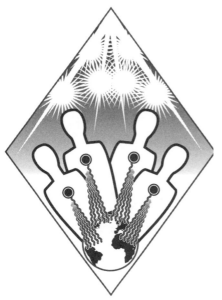

A Co-Creative Partnership Session

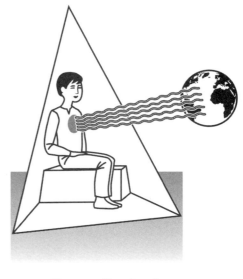

**Process Number 9
The Total Environment Process**

**Process Number 11
The Love and Light Process**

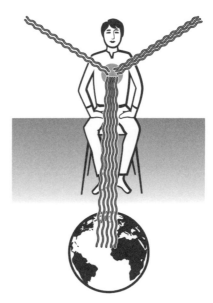

**Process Number 13
The Matrix**

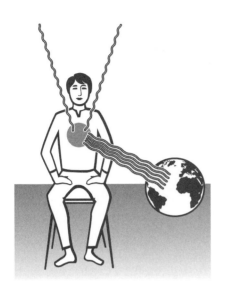

Process Number 14
The Light Process

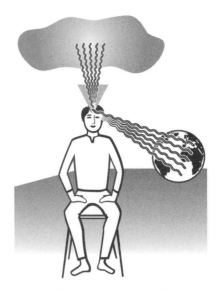

Process Number 15
Dynamic of Harmony and Well-Being

This is a sample of a counter-clockwise spinning geometric symbol

The Fifteen Processes

As these processes are executed, there will be two ways that this execution will take place. The first way is for nature to execute the process. The second way is for the human participant to call forth the energies. In either case, nature will execute the implementation of the process called for. Nature has the power to set into motion the required elements necessary for the proper installation of each process. Before each process, we will identify which partner will bring forth the energy called for—the human partner, nature, or both.

1. Preparing the Environment

Preparing the environment sets the stage for subsequent processes. Contained within this process are elements that remove any energies that no longer resonate with the advancing energies. The removal will dramatically shift the environment to a receptive state capable of bringing balance and well-being to the newly treated environment.

The purpose of this process is to bring the most extensive, coordinated reconstruction to any environment. As the environment receives the infusion of new elements, it will begin its coordinated journey into well-being. As the earth accepts the new energies presented in the Awakened Earth Processes, there will be significant change to the overall environment.

Once treated, an individual environment will have the capacity to come into greater balance and begin to function more optimally. This is being done so that the earth will have the fullest opportunity to align with forces now available to her.

This will give each environment a chance to reconfigure in a way that suits the overall changes the earth is making at this time in its evolution. The earth has, at its core, a desire for reconciliation with the inhabitants living upon it.

In order to fully work with all of these new processes, it will be necessary to begin by determining the amount of light that is present. This will be done by asking your team, "How much light does this property hold?" The answer will be determined by nature's assessment. In other words, you do not have to know, you only have to ask your team. Nature will respond by giving you a number between one and twelve. These numbers represent the amount of density that resides in any given piece of property. The amount of light will correspond to a specific geometric symbol, which is to be placed visually into the property you are working with. The amount of light determines which symbol is to be inserted into the property. Let us explain.

Each property carries a determined amount of density and of light. This is determined by the consciousness of the property. We have established the criteria for determining the amount of light and the amount of density. It is as follows:

Light and Symbols

For our purposes, we will be using five symbols that will be representative of the twelve symbols. It is not necessary to have the exact replica in mind. Nature will know.

If the light is a "1," then the symbol to be used will be a flat Triangle. This Triangle will be placed into the property during the visualization. If the light is a "2," then the symbol to be used will be a Tetrahedron. Each symbol will be will be placed into the property.

If the light is a "3," then the symbol to be used will be a Cube.

If the light is a "4," then the symbol to be used will be a Dodecahedron.

None of the above four symbols will spin.

If the light is a "5," then the symbol to be used is a Stellated Icosahedron. The Stellated Icosahedron will be placed into the property and, during the visualization, this geometric symbol will rotate counterclockwise.

If the light is a "6," then the symbol to be used is a Stellated Dodecahedron. The Stellated Dodecahedron will rotate counterclockwise.

If the light is a "7," then the symbol to be used is a Great Stellated Icosahedron. The Great Stellated Icosahedron will rotate counterclockwise.

If the light is an "8," then the symbol to be used is a Stellated Octahedron. The Stellated Octahedron will rotate counterclockwise.

If the light is a "9," then the symbol to be used is a Great Stellated Dodecahedron. The Great Stellated Dodecahedron will rotate counterclockwise.

If the light is a "10," then the symbol to be used is a Star Tetrahedron. The Star Tetrahedron will rotate counterclockwise.

If the light is an "11," then the symbol to be used is a Star Icosahedron. The Star Icosahedron will rotate counterclockwise.

If the light is a "12," then the symbol to be used is a Star Icosidodecahedron. The Icosidodecahedron will rotate counterclockwise.

The visualization does not have to be an exact replica of the symbol. Nature knows and will insert the symbol, which represents the amount of light.

Nature will execute this process.

To aid with the visualization process in the administering of some of the processes, we will illustrate five of the twelve symbols.

Illustrations for Five Geometric Symbols

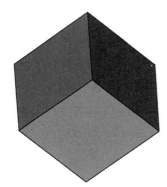

Symbol 1: Cube

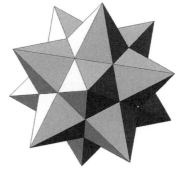

Symbol 2: Stellated Dodecahedron

Symbol 3: Star Icosahedron

Symbol 4: Tetrahedron

Symbol 5: Dodecahedron

The visualization does not have to be an exact replica of the symbol. Allow your imagination to fill in for the others. Nature knows and will insert the symbol that best represents the designated amount of light. Your role is to ask nature (your co-creative partnership) what amount of light is present in your environment. Some of the symbols are representative of more complex symbols and will serve as "stand-ins" for the more complex symbols. We assume you that know what a triangle looks like.

The Triangle is to be used when the light on the property measures one.

The Tetrahedron is to be used when the light on the property measures two.

The Cube is to be used when the light on the property measures three.

The Dodecahedron is to be used when the light on the property measures four.

The Stellated Dodecahedron is to be used whenever the light measures *five, six, or seven.* It will stand in for the Stellated Icosahedron and the Great Stellated Icosahedron. This design will serve for all three measures of light.

The Star Icosahedron will stand in for the Stellated Octahedron, the Great Stellated Dodecahedron, the Star Tetrahedron, and the Star Icosidodecahedron whenever the light measures *eight, nine, ten, eleven, or twelve.*

This design will serve for all five measures of light.

After you and your partnership determine the amount of light present on your environment, you will refer to the Light and Symbols Chart to determine correct symbol to use.

Example: You have identified that your property holds a light quotient of six. By referring to the Light and Symbols Chart, you see that the symbol for a light quotient of six is a Stellated Dodecahedron. In your visualization, you will place the Stellated Dodecahedron into the heart of the property. This symbol will rotate counter clockwise during your visualization.

Another example: You determine that your property holds the light quotient of seven. Even though the chart says to use a Great Stellated Icosahedron, you will visualize the Stellated Dodechedron. Nature knows how to make the adjustment and will insert the correct symbol. Again, this symbol will rotate counter clockwise.

Your job is to identify the accurate amount of light. During the visualization, nature will do the rest. These symbols are aids and will help you in administering the energies.

Authors Note: I *was unable to find suitable examples of the more intricate symbols for some of the corresponding light quotients. Nature worked out this formula for us to use.*

Light _____ **Symbol** _____

Be sure to allow for each process to settle into the environment by waiting a few moments after the completion of energy distribution. This will ensure that the environment has received the maximum benefit.

1. Center in your heart. Allow for the energy to come into alignment with the higher resonances present. When the energy is activated, visualize the universe as it opens in

your mind's eye. From the universe, visualize a green ray. Allow this ray to flow into your mind's eye and then into the property. Wait approximately *two minutes*. As the property fills with the green ray, the property will automatically close. This will prepare the property to receive the processes that follow.

2. Visualize a sheet that is placed underneath the entire property. Your partnership will automatically place the sheet at the designated depth. This will alert the property and the property will respond to the designated depth. Once the sheet is in place, begin to visualize the sheet rising up through the layers of soil, rock and sand. As the sheet rises, it will gather the energies that are no longer needed. Then it will release the energies to the greater universe.

3. Bring your attention back to the center of your heart. Once again allow the green ray to flow into your heart from the universe. Once the flow is established, turn your attention to the property. Visualize the property opening. Insert the specific geometric symbol into the property, based upon the amount of light on the property. Depending on the amount of light, determine if the symbol is to spin or not. Allow the green ray to flow through the geometric symbol and into the property so that the property is filled with the green ray. This flow will take approximately two minutes to complete. Verify when this is done.

4. As the green ray finishes its flow, allow the symbol to remain in place and immediately allow the flow of a gold ray into the property to begin, just as the green ray has

done. The gold ray also will flow through the geometric symbol and fill the property. This process, too, will take approximately **two minutes** to complete.

5. When the gold ray is complete in your mind's eye, remove the geometric symbol. Once again, allow the green ray to flow into the property. Allow this flow for *one minute.*

As this process concludes, there will be a significant shift within all life residing on the property. This process will have enabled the property to resume its function as a coherent life form and to be integrated into the larger environment in which it resides. Correspondingly, the surrounding environment will begin to come into harmony with the treated environment. Therefore, be mindful that, as you treat an environment, there will be changes to the surrounding environments as well. There will be a change in the larger environment as it incorporates the energies from the treated environment. In this way, greater and greater portions of the environment will be receiving these beneficial energies. As the environment is brought into balance, it will begin to take on the resonance of the new energies being delivered to the Earth.

2. The Collaboration Process

Each environment is a unique and definitive biosphere. Therefore, whenever these processes are introduced there will be significant changes to the surrounding environment. Each environment will receive whatever is needed to begin its alignment with the new energies. Once these energies have been introduced into the fabric of an environment, the environment will have the necessary structures to hold the incoming energies. Visualization is the method for delivering the collaboration process.

The human participant will execute this process.*

Before beginning this process, it is essential to determine the amount of light and the appropriate symbol to be utilized.

Light _____ **Symbol** _____

Setting the Stage

1. Bring your attention into the region of your heart. Center in the energy. In the heart center is the mechanism for conducting the energies needed to stabilize the environment. The heart mechanism is the place of initiation for bringing together the energies needed to insure that each property receives what it needs. As the heart activates, it will open frequencies that can harmonize the existing vibrations with the new vibrations.

---

* *(Whenever the human partner executes the process, nature's role is to hold the energies so that the human partner has nature's support while the energy is being distributed.)*

Once these energies are activated, the environment will move into a new frequency.

2. The property will self-identify the location of its center. The property will automatically open.

    Once the property has opened, use visualization to place the appropriate symbol into the property. The symbol will be determined by the amount of light on the property when you bring these energies to it. For example, if the light is a 5, the symbol to be inserted will be a Stellated Icosahedron. As you visualize a Stellated symbol, the unseen partners in this collaboration will insert the exact symbol indicated.

    Each property begins with a certain amount of light. With the infusion of these energetic components, the amount of light is likely to increase. Once the symbol has been identified, determined by the amount of light, it will be placed into the property. The amount of light will determine whether the symbol is to rotate or not. Refer to the Light and Symbol Chart for this information. As the symbol is placed into the property, it will rotate, or not, as determined by the amount of light. With the symbol in place, the next element to be introduced will be a color or colors.

    As the color or colors enter the symbol, they will be dispersed according to the amount of points existing in the symbol. As the light increases, so do the points on the symbols. For example, a Triangle has three points and does not rotate. A Stellated Icosahedron has fifteen points and will rotate.

3. The Color Balance

Calibration duration: Thirty seconds to four minutes
Infusion duration: Twenty to sixty seconds

Nature and the human partner execute the Calibration and the Infusion.

This process is designed to bring balance to the many levels that exist in any given environment. Color Balance is, in effect, a calibration of the total environment in order to synthesize all living matter. In the circumstances we are working with, it will be necessary to balance the environment using the single color red during the Infusion.

There are several factors to be considered in the Color Balance. The process begins with a Color Calibration.

1. Determine the duration of the Calibration.

2. Sit quietly while nature fulfills the Calibration.

3. The second part of the Color Balance is called the Infusion.

4. Determine the duration of the Color Infusion.

5. Allow the partnership to infuse the property with the color red.

6 Sit quietly while nature fulfills the Color Infusion.

4. Color Attunement Process

The purpose of the Color Attunement Process is to bring balance into the stated environment by using color in a specific way. This color process differs from the Color Balance Process in that it offers stabilization while, at the same time, bringing harmony into the environment. With this Color Attunement Process comes a new level of balance. This process will also enhance the overall vitality of the ecosystem.

The human partner executes this Color Attunement.*

Before beginning this process, it is essential to determine the amount of light and the appropriate symbol to be utilized.

Light _____ **Symbol** _____

1. Move your attention into your heart. Become aware of the resonance there.

2. Ask your partners which color or colors are to be inserted into the property. As you introduce the color or colors through the designated symbol, the amount of light will determine whether the symbol is to spin or not. The two choices of color are red, green, and gold combined or violet.

3. In your mind's eye, allow the chosen color or colors to flow through the symbol and into the center of the property. Visualize the symbol as it fills with the color or colors and is dispersed throughout the environment.

4. When the colors have finished flowing, remove the symbol and allow the property to close.

* *Refer to page 123.*

Witness the property for a few moments to sense any changes that may have occurred. This will anchor the energies and provide the needed support for the environment to stabilize more quickly.

5. Vibrational Attunement Process

Device Needed: A chromatic pitch instrument or "pitch pipe"
Purpose: To bring about the attunement of the entire environment

This process provides the balance needed to assist the environment to come into alignment with Earth's resonance. Specifically, there will be a measure of balance introduced by the sounds brought to the environment by the pitch instrument. In other words, this process serves to align the environment with the greater body of Earth. The tones are calibrated and will produce alignment throughout the many levels of life that exist in the environment.

Be sure to read through this process in its entirety before executing.

Nature executes the Vibrational Attunement Process.

Before beginning this process, be sure to determine the amount of light and the appropriate symbol to be utilized.

Light _____ **Symbol** _____

1. Using the pitch pipe, sound the tones for aligning the environment with the greater body of the earth. These tones will strengthen and harmonize the environment by aligning with each of the chakras of the individual property. In the event that an individual environment has undergone previous processes, there will be a noticeable amount of conditioning, which will be evident to your partnership. Also, there will be some resonance of the incorporated energies so that each process will build upon the other.

These processes will give a measure of stability to the existing energies, which have sustained great harm. Once the tones have been sounded, there will be a new resonance within the larger ecosystem. Each tone will resonate with the corresponding chakra within the environment that is being treated. The tones have the ability to synthesize the frequencies that are present in any given environment. The tones also add harmony to each environment.

2. Begin the process by bringing your awareness into your heart center. Align with the frequencies in your heart by sounding the tone "B," using a standard pitch pipe. This tone will alert the property and bring it into resonance with the newer energies. Concurrently, this will send a message to the greater universe to be ready to distribute its resonance into the environment that is being activated.

   Sound this tone for approximately fifteen seconds. Next, again bringing your awareness into the region of your heart, align your heart to the tone "A." With the pitch pipe, sound this tone for fifteen seconds. This will alert the heart of the property to resonate with the higher frequencies present in the environment. Give the property a chance to align with the tone that has just been sounded.

   Next, sound the tone "D" to align with the core of the property, which will bring it into alignment with the other frequencies already sounded. In order to bring further harmony to the other frequencies, it will be necessary to sound the rest of the tones in this sequence: "G," "A," and "C," each for approximately fifteen seconds. Next, sound the tone "F," also for approximately fifteen seconds; this note harmonizes all the tones that have been activated. As the tones are sounded, the environment will come into accord with the larger body of earth. This will help any property to withstand the bombardment of unusual frequencies. It will also strengthen the environment that is accepting them. Each tone represents a chakra that corresponds with the human chakra system. When the tones are sounded individually, they resonate with an individual chakra and come into alignment with the larger chakra system of earth. To reiterate, the tones are to be sounded in the following order: B, followed by A, followed by D, followed by G, followed by A, followed by C, and finally F.

3. When the tones have been sounded, there will be greater stability within each environment, allowing the environment to be receptive to the insertion of a geometric symbol.

4. The symbol chosen will be determined by the amount of light present in the individual property. This is determined by asking your unseen partners.

5. The property will make its preparations to receive the symbol. The center of the property will respond by opening to receive these energies.

6. When the symbol is inserted, using visualization, there will be an automatic response by the environment, enabling the induction of the energies. This will be done by dispersing the color through the geometric symbol as it flows into the property. By following the Light and Symbol Chart, you will know whether the symbol is to spin or not.

7. Determine with your team which choice of colors are to be used. The choices are: 1) a braiding of red, green, and gold or 2) violet. These are the two choices. No other colors are to be used. As you insert the symbol into the property you will release the color or colors into the geometric symbol. This will allow for each symbol to be a conduit for the color that has been selected and will reduce the amount of imbalance. In each case, the geometric symbol selected will spin if the designated amount of light is greater than "four." If the designated amount of light is "four" or less, the geometric symbol will remain stationery and will not rotate. When the color is provided, there will be a new resonance operating within each property to bring harmony and balance.

8. The flow of color will last for approximately six minutes. Be sure to verify with the team that this process is complete. At this time, through visualization, you will remove the geometric symbol and allow the property to close.

9. Your Awakened Earth partners will harness the power of these colors and disperse the color throughout the environment. They also will infuse the environment with many other substances that are compatible with the needs of the individual environment. These substances are infused into the environment in a way that provides maximum stability. Given the short amount of time needed by the Awakened Earth collaboration to complete this process, the work can easily be accomplished within a half-hour.

6. Infusion of New Energy

Duration: Two to four minutes

Nature and the human partner execute the Infusion of New Energy.

The Foundation for Activating the Processes

Many of the processes serve to align an environment with the greater field of expression. In many cases, there will be additional processes introduced into an environment. While the environment is assimilating the infusion of energies from several of the processes, there will be additional changes taking place. The new and refined energies will begin to bring harmony and balance to the environment. As these processes are implemented, they will begin the process of strengthening and stabilizing the treated environment. The earth will begin to respond and will come into resonance with the greater environment surrounding it. The earth has the ability to come into resonance with the emerging energies so that it will maximize its strength and stability.

The infusion of the New Energy Process will enable the earth to begin to regain its stability and balance in order to harmonize with the greater cosmos. The earth has come into a place of receptivity. With the Awakened Earth Project, the earth will move into alignment with the greater cosmos. What was once considered to be a planet of humanity will be known as the planet of Oneness. These processes serve as a foundation for the earth to be in alignment with the larger field of expression.

This process will deliver foundational energies that have been infused with elements necessary for the environment to align with more sophisticated energies. The goal of this process is to harmonize the energies so that each environment will receive what is needed for maximum stabilization. Harmonized energies will give the environment what is needed in order to balance the frequencies that already reside there.

Following this infusion, there will be a period of adjustment as the new energies mingle with the existing energies in the environment. The Awakened Earth Masters will determine the duration of the infusion, after which there will be a period of time when these energies settle in. As the Awakened Earth Project unfolds, the earth will respond by assimilating more and more of the new energies so that there will be changes to earth's overall balance. This shift in the overall balance will be between the new frequencies and the existing frequencies.

The energy infusion will prepare the environment to hold a higher frequency. This will allow the environment to house the new energy comfortably. With intention and the application of the new energy into your environment, the environment will begin to transform. The new energy that has been introduced into an environment will take on the properties of the existing environment and will transform it.

Steps for the Infusion of New Energy

1. Ask the Awakened Earth Masters to determine the duration for the Infusion of New Energy Process.

2. With visualization, let the energy move into the property or environment you are working with. As this energy mixes with

the existing energy on the property, there will be a period of adjustment. While the environment assimilates the new energy, wait quietly until the assimilation is complete.

3. Verify that the assimilation process is complete.

7. The Harmony Process

Duration: One to six minutes

The Harmony Process is designed to bring harmony into any environment. This process has the power to eliminate discord and restore balance. It will also alleviate imbalances that are detrimentally impacting the overall environment. As the Harmony Process is introduced, there will be additional movement throughout the entire ecosystem. As this movement occurs, there will be a new resonance existing in the larger ecosystem. These harmonious energies will introduce the elements needed for the environment to begin to come into balance. They will also deliver a higher frequency. This will allow the environment to accommodate a more sophisticated and complex energy.

Nature will execute the Harmony Process.

1. Determine the duration. It will be between one and six minutes.

2. Place your awareness into the center of your heart. Feel the harmony that is present. Center in the energy you find there.

3. Move your awareness to the place or environment that has been readied for The Harmony Process.

4. Invite the environment to receive the benefit of harmony.

5. Open your heart and proceed to allow the energy of harmony to flow. After a period of from one to six minutes, this process will be complete.

6. Nature will bring harmony to the environment.

7. Wait quietly for this to be fulfilled.

Note: Ask your partners if the Dynamic of Harmony and Well-being is to be used in conjunction with The Harmony Process. Refer to page 123 for further explanation.

8. Exchange of Energy Process

The human partner will execute the process.*

The transfer will be instantaneous.

In order to successfully use this process, you will need to be in a state of balance.

1. Begin by centering in your heart. This will align your frequencies with the higher frequencies. Wait for approximately sixty seconds for this alignment to occur.

2. When you are centered, bring your attention into the environment you will be working with. This will activate the environment and make it ready to receive the energies. Using the power of visualization, enter the place you are addressing. The environment will respond by preparing itself to receive the energetic transfer.

3. In order to successfully transfer the intention to the property, bring your attention to it. This will allow the property to move into alignment with the intention. Because your focus is in harmony, as a result of centering in your heart, the property will automatically align with the energy of harmony.

---

* *Refer to page 123.*

9. Total Environment Balance

Duration of balance: Two to six minutes
Duration of stabilization: Fifteen seconds

The human and nature partners will jointly execute this process.

In order to provide the maximum stability to an environment, the Total Environment Balance is utilized. This will enhance the environment's ability to maintain an ongoing stability. An individual environment will have the ability to come into balance, once this process is utilized. What is required of you is to ask the unseen to do so. Your partners will distribute the elements necessary for the environment to come into balance.

1. Determine the duration of the Total Environment Balance.

2. Ask your partners to prepare the environment to receive the energies. Wait for ten seconds; this will open the pathways for the frequencies to be incorporated into the existing energy field. In this way, all of the contributing energies will be transferred as a unit into the environment. The environment will incorporate this new and refined energy and will become stabilized as it assimilates the new energies. This process will take from *two to six minutes.* Sit quietly while nature does this work. The environment will come into alignment with its highest nature.

3. Ask nature to bring stabilization to the environment. Wait approximately *fifteen seconds* for this to be completed.

4. Stabilization will occur automatically.

Note: Ask your partners if the Dynamic of Harmony and Well-being is to be used in conjunction with the Total Environment Balance. Refer to page 123 for further explanation.

10. The Calibration Process

Duration: Forty-five seconds to four minutes

Nature will execute this process.

The unseen will calibrate the environment by using techniques that are aligned with the higher forces. This calibration will serve several purposes. First, it will unify all the levels of life that are in existence in the given environment. Second, it will provide support to the many levels of life that are not apparent to the human eye. In doing so, there will be a further unification of the matter and content of all life residing in the environment. For example, in an ecosystem that has received the Awakened Earth Processes, there will be an influx of energies that are new to the environment. Third, there will be sufficient new matter infused into the environment, which will bring about significant change on many levels of life.

1. Ask the Awakened Earth Masters to reveal the duration of the calibration.

2. Sit quietly while this calibration is performed.

3. Verify that this is complete.

Note: Ask your partners if the Dynamic of Harmony and Well-being is to be used in conjunction with The Calibration Process. Refer to page 123 for further explanation.

11. The Love and Light Process

Duration: Two to six minutes

The human partner will execute this process.*

The purpose of The Love and Light Process is to bring the environment the benefits of greater harmony. In doing so, the environment will begin to regain its stability. As this process has the potential to bring harmony into a wide range of situations, it must be applied with the understanding that it can alter circumstances. Situations that can be helped with the Love and Light Process include environments that are having difficulty coming into balance and any environment that requires human help, using these methods.

1. Determine the duration of the Love and Light Process.

2. Bring your attention into your heart.

3. Allow the heart mechanism time to become centered in love. This will bring the resonances into alignment with other vibrations that are coming into harmony with the love in your heart center. Wait approximately ten seconds for this connection to occur.

4. Once the generator in the heart is activated, bring your attention to the place of difficulty (Environments, systems, or any other situation).

5. With intention, allow for the resonances to move into the place of difficulty. The heart will automatically close as the flow finishes.

---

* *Refer to page 123.*

12. Frequency Stabilization Process

Duration: Always sixty seconds

Purpose: To bring balance to situations that are not responding to other methods

The human and nature partners will jointly execute this process.

The Frequency Stabilization Process will offer significant help to any environment. Situations that can benefit from Frequency Stabilization are: environments that have begun to deteriorate, situations that have not been resolved through conventional means, and issues that need further assistance. For example, when an environment is experiencing difficulty coming into balance through other methods, the Frequency Stabilization can provide the means.

1. Align yourself with the energies of the heart by bringing your attention inward.

2. Hold the vision of the environment coming into balance for sixty seconds.

13. The Matrix

Duration: Approximately six minutes

The human partner will execute this process.*

Together with humanity, the unseen will begin to incorporate the finer frequencies that are currently available into the fabric of earth's resonance. Gradually, there will be an increase in the earth's resonance. The new resonance has the capacity to bring about an enlightened state of consciousness. The Matrix will provide suitable amounts of light and distribute them in a manner that conforms to the natural order. The Matrix has within it the code for the earth to become aligned with its higher counterpart in the larger cosmos. It also gives the earth the needed light to accelerate its path toward becoming the center of the universe.

Conditions for Using the Matrix

We urge care and discretion in using the Matrix. The Matrix will generate a finer amount of light, which will begin to dissolve the existing imbalanced conditions. When this happens, there will be a corresponding amount of light readily available to bring harmony into the existing environment. The Matrix will provide the needed support to allow an environment to come into greater balance. The Matrix is an acceleration to establish greater balance.

The precautions are as follows: The Matrix is only to be used when designated by the Awakened Earth Masters. Once the Matrix has been identified as a suitable means to equip an

---

* *Refer to page 123.*

environment with light, nature and the Masters will organize the energy so that it can be distributed by the partnership.

1. Determine the duration of the Matrix.

2. Bring your attention into the heart. Become aware of the energy that has coalesced there.

3. Bring your attention to the environment that is being resistant to acclimating to the new energy. Visualize the property opening to receive the new energy.

4. Allow the energy in your heart to flow to the identified property. When the flow of energy is complete, it will automatically cease to flow.

5. The opening to the property will automatically close.

14. The Light Process

Duration: Forty-five seconds to six minutes

The human partner will execute this process.*

The Light Process will bring an exceptional amount of light into any environment. To facilitate the dispersing of the light frequencies, the Awakened Earth Masters will distribute the needed light by using a new delivery system. This system has the power to infuse any situation with light. What is more, when this process is utilized, there will be a substantially greater impact on the adjoining energy fields. When this occurs the existing energy fields will no longer continue as before. They will cease to function as the unit they once were.

Once this process is used, there will be a new field of existence incorporated into the larger environment. This will give the larger environment the opportunity to come into a more cohesive balance. All that is in the property will be in alignment with the new field of existence. Once these energies have been delivered through the Light Process, the environment will hold the new frequency.

The Light Process has the potential to bring significant change to existing environments by strengthening the overall balance within the environment. Once the environment has received the energy from this process, there will be a noticeable difference in the way the existing field responds to the new energy.

1. Determine the duration for the Light Process.

2. Bring your attention into the heart. As the energy expands, let the heart chakra open. This will allow the energy to move with ease to the environment.

3. With your awareness, visualize the energy moving into the selected environment.

4. The heart chakra will automatically close as the flow finishes.

15. The Dynamic of Harmony and Well-being Process

Duration: One to four minutes

This process can be used alone or in conjunction with other Awakened Earth processes. The human and nature partners will jointly execute this process.

The Dynamic of Harmony and Well-being Process has within it the capacity for bringing a new order to any environment. As this occurs, the environment will begin to resonate in a manner that is conducive to bringing the environment to the state of well-being necessary for health.

1. Ask your partners to determine the duration of this process.

2. Call on the Dynamic of Harmony and Well-being. This will activate several dynamics, including the resonance of Harmony and Well-being. Wait ten seconds for this activation to occur.

3. Once this activation has occurred, bring your awareness into a place of peace where you will have access to other dimensions. At this place of intersection with the higher dimensions, you will start the flow of Harmony and Well-being.

4. When the flow is complete, the energy will automatically stop.

The Added Role of the Dynamic of Harmony and Well-being

** To determine if the Dynamic of Harmony and Well-being is to be used in conjunction with other Awakened Earth Processes, you will ask the Awakened Earth Masters if it is appropriate. They may recommend that the Dynamic of Harmony and Well-being be used along with Processes #7, #9, or #10. This fortification will supply additional strength to the other processes. At this time, Processes # 7, # 9, and # 10 are the only processes to be used in conjunction with the Dynamic of Harmony and Well-being. The inclusion of the Dynamic of Harmony and Well-being with any other process is to be used only at the discretion of the Awakened Earth Masters. It is NOT to be included otherwise.

* Whenever the human partner executes the process, nature's role is to hold the energies so that the human partner has nature's support while the energy is being distributed.

A Summary of the Processes

Once these processes have been introduced into an environment, there will be a coalescing of energies that will provide the impetus needed for an environment to begin its return to health. The Awakened Earth model will open the way for the existing environment to be brought into harmony with its more aligned and integrated whole. Once this has happened, a greater amount of light will be present, which will bring more balance to the existing environment. The Light Process, along with the other processes, has the potential to reverse decades of deterioration and bring health and balance to these jeopardized environments.

All environments, when treated using these advanced measures, will begin to rebuild and rejuvenate in harmony and balance. We are noting many environments that are having difficulty staying in balance. We are confident that, once these energies take hold, many environments will come back into balance. As we have said throughout the descriptions of the Awakened Earth processes, the earth has agreed to the influx of these supportive energies.

The Awakened Earth began as an outgrowth of an active interest in the environment. What was originally a call to bring balance to individual environments quickly became a much more coordinated effort to create a new model for a co-creative means to bring balance to larger areas of earth. The environment has withstood many assaults over decades of mistreatment. But with the emergence of the Awakened Earth, there are significant reasons to be optimistic.

These processes have been designed to bring help to an environment without disturbing any ongoing life forms within that environment. We have witnessed improvement to many different environments that have received the benefit of these processes. As we anticipate the tide turning, because of the application of these processes, we are mindful that the earth has beckoned humanity into a co-creative endeavor that has no precedent in human history. While it is yet unknown to what extent the earth will benefit, there can be no doubt that the earth will gain significantly with the introduction of the Awakened Earth model.

In keeping with our initial intention, we, the Awakened Earth Masters, are standing by in hopes that our efforts will be received in the spirit of care and compassion for the earth that we love.

As we embark on this momentous journey, we are cognizant of the possibilities that lie ahead. We are more than ready to partner with you. We have held this day in our hearts and beings for many millennia. The time has come to birth a new generation of co-creation.

Section Two

After the Awakened Earth Movement Begins

CHAPTER 7

The Earth Responds

The earth has been conditioned to adjust to the changes currently taking place. But as the planet adjusts to energetic changes as well as physical ones, there will be a need to offer support, so that the earth can come into balance and stability. What this means, in the short term, is that the earth will begin to respond to the introduction of energies presented by The Awakened Earth processes.

The Awakened Earth has the potential to give the earth adequate support as she transitions into her assigned role as the *Central Sun for the entire cosmos. As we enter into a new era, there will be some fundamental changes to be supported. One of these changes will be the ability to work directly with the Awakened Earth Masters. Also, a broader understanding has emerged as a result of the Awakened Earth model of co-creation.

---

* Central Sun is the term used by the Ascended Masters to describe the function the earth will perform as life evolves. It refers to the magnanimous step earth is making at this juncture in her evolution process.

The earth, in her wisdom, is aware of the changes that need to be made. She has agreed, as part of her evolution, to partner with humanity.

The earth is a living, breathing body of life. She has been, up until now, the recipient of much misunderstanding. The earth has agreed to work with those of you who are dedicated to establishing partnerships in order to reestablish harmony and balance throughout the earth.

As this course is presented to the world, there will be some who are certain to find fault with the premise of using co-creative partnerships to solve some of these pressing problems. However, it will be shown that this endeavor can indeed, deliver. As we continue to use these processes, we will gain evidence that these applications are having an overall beneficial impact on specific environments. That evidence will lessen the naysayer considerably.

We are in the business of serving the earth. According to our projections, there will be significant interest in this Awakened Earth model from those who are dedicated to helping the earth, and especially those who are aware of the spiritual underpinnings of this concept. These will be people who are interested in and devoted to serving the higher good.

The Awakened Earth Masters will not entertain those who serve only their own interests. We will not cooperate with them. We will not engage in partnerships with those whose intent is self-serving. This is a project solely for those who will invest time and expertise on behalf of earth and her inhabitants. We will assist those of you who have shown to be reliable stewards of the earth and those of you who come to this work in earnest.

**The conditions for participating in a co-creative partnership
are:**

1. Demonstrate a willingness to serve the earth.

2. Align with the co-creative principles presented in the
    Awakened Earth model.

3. Bring an open mind.

4. Prepare to be engaged in a co-creative partnership.

5. Offer yourself in reverence to the earth.

For our common purpose, will you consider your availability,
based on the criteria stated above? If you can meet these criteria,
you may be a match for the Awakened Earth project. We trust
you will be forthright in your heart. There is far too much at
stake for misuse to be allowed. With that stated, we welcome
you into this far-reaching endeavor.

As you make the decision to join the Awakened Earth, let us
remind you that you may be committing to a period of at least six
months to bring balance to any environment with which you choose
to work. When you sign on to this project, you will be entering a
school of epic proportions. You will be in training with a host of
Masters who have agreed to teach you how to work co-creatively.

We have already entered into partnership with some of you.
Others of you, who are coming to this material by way of intuition,
may find yourselves drawn to this project. However, that does not
mean you are exempt from meeting the stated criteria. Most likely
you are well aware of the profound nature of this work.

As we enter the realm of co-creation, let us remind you that
you are investing your time in a comprehensive course designed

to help you reclaim the environment. This course of study is designed by nature and Masters who are equipped to deliver measures never before used for the benefit of the earth. We are offering training that is profound in its scope and the possibilities it presents. We have the utmost faith in its outcome. We are confident that, once you have experienced its power, you will agree.

Nature, along with the Masters, has the power to rebalance any situation, given the benefit of these Awakened Earth energies. Once you have witnessed the dramatic improvements as these processes are engaged, you will realize they are nothing short of miraculous.

Our calculations suggest that, once these Awakened Earth energies have been introduced worldwide, there will be an aggregate accumulation of balanced energy entering the earth's atmosphere. This, itself, will cause change. According to our calculations, the Awakened Earth will help bridge the divide currently in existence by offering a balanced energy. But in order for the earth to come into balance, there will need to be a concerted effort to offer the earth the energies needed by incorporating the Awakened Earth model into environments across the globe.

As these energies are introduced, there will be some shifts in the amount of light penetrating the earth's atmosphere. As we proceed with this introduction of energy, there is likely to be an overall increase in light throughout the entire universe. As we have said, this project holds the key to harmonizing the entire planet, as long as the Awakened Earth is handled with care and respect.

Once the earth has adjusted to the influx of these finer energies, there will be an increase in the amount of some of the more refined energy, which will be making its way into the earth's atmosphere. These finer energies have the capacity to usher in harmonious energy, provided that their introduction is gradual and supervised. This supervision is something we are prepared to do. By supervision, we mean that we, of nature, are prepared to blend the energies so that they will be compatible with the existing environment. This will increase the earth's ability to function in a more balanced manner. What this means in layman's terms is that the earth has the ability to accommodate a higher resonance.

As these energies are introduced, there will be a need for some of you to align the higher frequencies with the greater atmosphere. This work will be accomplished by some of you who know how to work with the larger universe and can take on this project in your partnership.

Earth Is a Deliberate Consciousness

Many of you realize that we are entering an age of enlightenment. During this age, there will be several new mechanisms available to assess the condition of the environment. Currently, there is one organization capable of examining the conditions of environments across the world. The National Oceanic and Atmospheric Association gives uniform reports whenever there is a change to the way the earth is behaving. It gives the most current data available for assessing the environment and the earth as a whole.

According to the latest research by the National Oceanic and Atmospheric Association, there have been issues regarding how the earth is handling the increase in carbon dioxide. The data suggests that more carbon dioxide is leaking into the atmosphere by way of the hole in the ozone layer. The earth has had to adjust to increasing amounts of carbon dioxide while at the same time expelling the excess amounts. This is hampering the quest for clean air.

This double-edged sword is wreaking havoc among certain scholars, who are adamant in their belief that there will be catastrophic consequences if the ozone hole continues to expand. While this may be true, it does not present the danger some schools of thought might suggest.

In the short term, weather disturbances caused by the increasing ozone will begin to have an effect on the general weather patterns. Climate change has become a buzz-word that seeks to harness the power of fear, in order to gain favor for the earth. In keeping with the global response to climate change, we are prepared to advise and cooperate with those of you interested in partnering with us, to ensure that the earth can indeed come into balance for the purpose of sustaining viable health.

As the earth adjusts to the coming times, we are in a position to become partners with this planet and its residents. We can help to establish earth's viability and communicate her desire for balance. Think of it this way: the earth has a consciousness and is capable of determining certain outcomes for herself. As earth moves into juxtaposition with her sister planets, she has the capacity for evolving.

The planet's evolution is a given. What is not a given is her capacity to continue her support of humanity. In other words, earth is at a crossroads in her relationship with humanity. The time has come for humanity to realize its impact on the natural world.

Once I understood the impact the Awakened Earth project could have throughout the world, I began in earnest to complete this book. I established a network of people who could help me refine the processes and give the earth an opportunity to experience them. Now, however, I find myself at the brink of ushering this movement to the world. It goes without saying that I am in awe of the opportunity before us. Never in our human history has such an opportunity been available. We have before us a model of co-creation unlike any other, a model that can change our history and give us a balanced earth. Within the Awakened Earth project are the seeds to bring not only balance, but health to the earth. Can you imagine my excitement as this movement becomes reality? Nowhere on earth is there an opportunity to match this one!

Hurricanes Offer an Example

September, 2008

During the 2008 hurricane season, we had opportunities to monitor two different hurricanes: Ike and Gustav. Ike demonstrated the power and ferocity of a typical hurricane. Hurricanes are, by nature, storms that gain momentum while traveling over warm waters, where they increase in velocity and become major hurricanes. Ike did not have the benefit of receiving help from the Awakened Earth processes. As a result, the coastal areas in and around Galveston, Texas were flooded and many buildings were lost.

The energy present in Hurricane Ike was neither harmonious nor balanced. Without this inherent balance, the land could not sustain itself, so it gave way to the predictable forces. "Nature" had its way. However, "nature" was not the governing factor—humanity was. The shoreline was unprotected and heavily populated. Nature was out of balance. As a result, there were losses beyond measure. Nature can offer itself to humanity as a conduit for balance. But in the case of Ike, there was insufficient opportunity for nature to offer its balance.

As the storm approached, the natural resources along Galveston Bay were decimated and could offer little or no protection to the inhabitants of this coastal area. There were no manmade barriers capable of holding the water back; the wall along the shoreline offered little protection and gave false hope that it could do so. The hurricane bore down on Galveston, coming ashore with fervor. There was little chance for the buildings to survive. It was soon apparent that no amount of ingenuity could have saved Galveston. Nature simply was unable to stabilize the area. We believe that, if Galveston had received the benefit of the Awakened Earth processes, the impact from hurricane Ike would have been much less.

In contrast, Hurricane Gustav behaved in a much more balanced manner. The area over which Gustav traveled had received energy from Awakened Earth processes as early as 2005. During Hurricane Katrina, the Awakened Earth energies were first introduced to this area. This meant that the land was much more balanced before Gustav made landfall. In addition, Awakened Earth processes were utilized to stabilize the area surrounding New Orleans as Gustav approached.

The difference between Ike and Gustav is vast. Ike behaved in a predictable manner; Gustav did not. Gustav became a hurricane and then was downgraded before it was to become a hurricane again. The reason it was downgraded was because the water over which it traveled had been the recipient of the Awakened Earth processes. These processes gave Gustav the balance needed to bring down the wind speed and to alter its course several times.

Gustav was a beneficiary of the balanced energy produced by the insertion of the Awakened Earth process, Harmony. Both the land and the storm were given a Total Environment Balance. Subsequently, Gustav was able to recalibrate as a storm and deliver a much more balanced energy. The land upon which Gustav came ashore was sufficiently balanced because of prior applications of the Awakened Earth processes in 2005; because of this, much of New Orleans was spared a second severe blow. What is more, we have determined that, once these Awakened Earth processes are delivered to an environment, the subsequent offerings of these processes bring even greater balance to the overall environment.

What this means to those of you drawn to this material is that you can now bring balance into many environments and give these environments new life. The possibility to directly and favorably impact scores of environments across the globe lies within the pages of this book and within the model of the Awakened Earth.

Bringing Balance to Diverse Issues

This project is an unprecedented attempt to reverse decades of abuse and mismanagement. It is well within the reach of this generation to provide the next generation with a balanced earth. Doing so will be one of the single greatest achievements ever to be undertaken on behalf of earth. This endeavor will provide a template for humanity, as long as the processes presented herein are followed exactly as written. Each partnership will be a contributor to the earth's vitality and balance.

We are at a precipice in human development. Never before in history have there been as many serious challenges as there are today. But there also has never been a time of more opportunity. The seeds of the future lie in today. Measures are being introduced around the world to help humanity come to terms with the imbalances that exist everywhere.

When it is discovered that the Awakened Earth contains part of the solution, there will be a collective sigh of relief. Many will scoff at the notion of co-creative partnerships; nevertheless, such partnerships are irrefutably sound. The processes have been tried and tested. Evidence is accumulating that points to the viability of the Awakened Earth processes to deliver outstanding results.

Take for example, the measures on behalf of earth undertaken by a group of dedicated women, who were convinced that these processes could and would make a difference. They were right. They did make a difference. The earth has responded and welcomed the influx of the Awakened Earth energies. These women have established a foundation to build upon. The stage has been set. The earth is ready. What is needed is for partnerships to form and take these processes to areas across the globe. The opportunity is here. The opportunity is now.

While the Awakened Earth can and will bring balance to multiple situations, much depends upon the willingness of humanity to seek solutions capable of bringing balance, using the methods in this model. It is an endeavor whose potential is waiting to be tapped.

The intention of the Awakened Earth is to bring balance and harmony to distressed environments throughout the world. With this in mind, realize that the damage has been decades in the making and the reversal will take some time to accomplish. What is more, there will be times of slow progress and times of exceptional progress. This is to be expected as we weave together components to establish a healthy balance and one that can be maintained.

As we build upon the earlier successes, which have already been established, we will gain a more reliable base of knowledge. Given that we are in the pursuit of harmony and balance, it is important to point out there will be times of imbalance. These processes may encounter some stalls and setbacks along the way, but we know they will ultimately succeed.

As we continue to monitor the partnerships, we will determine how best to serve the whole Awakened Earth. We expect that, as these processes gradually become available on a wider scale, the earth will come into balance more quickly. At this point in time, there cannot be an accurate assessment as to the overall success. There are too many variables.

The earth has responded favorably to the earlier attention given to the Gulf Coast. Since hurricane Gustav, there has been significant reduction in flooding. What this means to us, as we observe the greater environment, is that the Awakened Earth is making a significant contribution to the recovery of these damaged Gulf coastlines. It has been apparent that, once an environment has received the energy from the Awakened Earth, the environment will take on attributes that contribute to the overall balance of the earth's environment. As time goes on, it will be verifiable that the introduction of the Awakened Earth processes will help the environment develop more balance.

CHAPTER 8

Nature Expands Its Horizons

A s I was preparing to bring this book into a usable format, I was struck by the significance of the co-creative process I was utilizing. Never before had I found such ease in establishing a partnership with the unseen. It was as if we were in dialogue, much in the same way that I would hold a conversation on the telephone. The distance between me and my partners was infinitesimal. I was soon able to recognize the coordination and flow between us as if we were joined by a common channel.

I realized then that I had learned to translate the information from my silent partners by tuning into their essences. They have also tuned into mine. This gives us the ability to converse in what is an almost seamless conversation. Of course, this has happened over time, but it has happened. I am sure this possibility exists for you, too.

Be patient. You are learning a new skill. The value of such communication cannot be underestimated.

The communication issue is at the forefront of all co-creative partnerships. In this endeavor, we are seeking a means of communication

141

that is advantageous to both nature and humanity. Whenever you engage in an Awakened Earth partnership, you will be activating an environment suitable for communicating with greater ease. This project has been conceived co-creatively and serves as a model by utilizing communication that is aligned with nature and completely within the framework of co-creation.

Nature Explains Nature

As we endeavor to bring you a product that is both useful and understandable, we have had to adjust our thinking to include the human mind. While this may seem an easy feat, it is not. We are accustomed to expressing ourselves in a manner of simplicity, and yet have realized that our understanding is different from yours. For example, when we say align with nature, we are referring to the *consciousness* of nature and not simply the trees.

From a human perspective, nature is a vast and powerful force of mystery. It does not conspire to destroy, although some forces of nature, such as the hurricanes, can be quite destructive. That nature intends destruction is a human interpretation. Nature is an organization of benevolence and is capable of bringing great joy to humanity. We are a consciousness of great compassion and reverence for life. We have come to understand life from a human perspective, which gives us a more informed perspective.

As a consciousness, we are capable and eager to bring balance to environments throughout the world. We have gone to great lengths to form partnerships with humanity so that we can help the world in these times of great change. What was once thought to be impossible now will be possible, because of the Awakened Earth project.

Nature has the capacity to align with humanity and begin the journey to oneness. In oneness, nature meets humanity as an equal. Nature will forever be grateful for humanity's willingness to join with us in service to the whole of life. We are exceptionally gratified for the opportunity that the Awakened Earth makes possible.

In this endeavor, we have attempted to bridge the communication barriers by introducing the expanded pendulum responses. These have given us a way to communicate more accurately between levels of thought. Take, for example, the usage of common words that can mean different things to different people. Unless the words are defined, there is little understanding. Moreover, as we move into an era of common thought, it becomes essential to have a reliable set of communication tools.

As a consciousness, we have no need for language. We operate in a field of existence that has no bounds. Our language is, by and large, a product of yours. You, however, are more constrained by the nature of the physical dimension. We have found the pendulum with the expanded responses to be the most viable way to communicate between the seen and the unseen.

In the formation of co-creative partnerships, we acknowledge that we have differences in understanding. However, for our purposes, there is one standard of co-creative partnership. It is established by the setting of an intention. As we have said, the intention serves as the form and the function of any co-creative partnership. The intention holds the blueprint for fulfillment by the co-creative partnership.

We have designed a workable format for the implementation of the intention. It is in compliance with the natural order and, therefore, in alignment with the higher order. So you can see, we have come together for the purpose of serving the greater good.

Further Issues To Be Addressed

As the Awakened Earth project is launched, there will be some issues that require urgent attention. Flooding has become one of the more urgent issues to address, because in many regions across the globe, it is taking its toll on the human condition. For example, when the Chinese people were evacuated after a recent flood event, their homes were demolished, leaving them homeless. This toll has been exacerbated by illness that is spreading across many parts of inland China. Recent flooding in Turkey and Greece is contributing to instability to the region. As Turkey and Greece are important sea ports, both these nations' commerce has been affected by the recent floods.

Some other important issues are: balancing the entire ecosystem affected by Hurricane Gustav; bringing balance to areas of neglect during the recent earthquakes in China; addressing the fire areas in the western United States; bringing balance to the wetlands of coastal New Zealand; balancing the weather extremes in North America; and creating harmony in the Alaskan Wildlife Refuge.

Additional environments suitable for treatment by the Awakened Earth fall into a political category. Nevertheless, these are environments. These areas of concern are: creating harmony and balance throughout Mediterranean countries seeking to become members of the United Nations; bringing harmony and balance to portions of the Middle East consumed by war; contributing balance to the Eastern Bloc Nations; harmonizing the interior portions of

Tibet; creating balance in the regions of Africa where genocide is rampant; distributing harmony throughout the Balkans; bringing balance to the regions of Israel that have sustained great harm; and bringing balance to the rainforests of Brazil.

These environments, while not conventional environments, can be treated using the Awakened Earth model. This expanded list of environments serves to open your thinking beyond the conventional understanding of environment.

Onset of New Energies

In this time of great change, there are new energies coming into the earth's atmosphere. These energies are bringing with them additional elements to help humanity transition from a third-dimensional reality to a more sophisticated, fifth-dimensional reality.

In the fifth dimension, there are elements and systems guaranteed to help humanity move forward with greater ease and stability. Gradually, as the new energies are assimilated, the existing environment will house a more refined energy. Secondly, the refined energies will be distributed throughout the environment, bringing to it a more refined balance. As this distribution of energy is thoroughly integrated into the existing environment, the environment will become more stable and capable of holding a higher resonance.

As the Awakened Earth formula is incorporated into the overall atmosphere of the earth, there will be significant changes to the biosphere. First of all, there is likely to be an increase in the way in which the earth assimilates the new energy coming into its atmosphere. Further, there will be an acceleration of harmonious energy that has been delivered by the Awakened Earth processes. As the processes are incorporated throughout the world, the energy they hold will contribute to the overall assimilation of the new energies making their way to earth. Because the Awakened Earth energies are balanced and harmonious, they will prepare the earth to assimilate the new, approaching energies.

The Awakened Earth will begin to bring these balanced energies into the larger environment. Together, the new energies coming into earth's atmosphere and the energies deposited by the Awakened Earth will coalesce and offer a more viable energetic foundation for the earth. As this happens, there will be a greater assimilation of balanced energy into the larger ecosystem.

Each treated environment will give the earth the added momentum to advance its core stability and bring balance into more and more environments. Gradually, as the Awakened Earth movement spreads across the globe, there will be added balance to the earth's stability and to its capability to bring health to environments worldwide.

As we begin to launch the Awakened Earth to the world, there will be a need for some of you reading this material to form your partnerships and begin to administer the Awakened Earth processes. For this project to be successful, we hope there will be a significant number of partnerships formed. These initial partnerships will form the foundation for future partnerships. With the introduction of these partnerships, we anticipate an expansion of the Awakened Earth project. This will hasten the integration of the incoming energies and give environments the boost they need.

Bringing Together Co-Creation with Substance

In the beginning of this project, there were conditions on the earth that warranted a new approach. We needed to address the rampant imbalances occurring throughout the world. These conditions gave rise to a need for interventions that could have an immediate effect without subjecting the earth to further imbalance.

The earth began responding favorably to the initial infusions of energy, which gave us reason to believe other infusions would do the same. Uniformly, the environments treated with the Awakened Earth processes were responding in ways that were new. The fabric of environments were coming into balance and holding energies in a substantively new way. These environments were coming to a place of balance in accordance with the natural order of the universe. The environments were holding functional patterns that were aligned with harmony and balance.

This was new for the earth. These environments were coming into a new balance as a direct result of the energies given to them by the Awakened Earth processes. We took note and soon realized that we were viewing an entirely new phenomenon. At this point, we decided to invest ourselves fully in the Awakened Earth. Throughout the journey of this project, we have kept a vigilant watch on the treated environments and found an enduring balance.

In the spring of 2009, we witnessed the return of abundant rainfall to the southernmost regions of the Appalachians. The three-year drought had been interrupted. That region has come into a harmonic balance, which is entirely new. This region will be a bellwether for the Awakened Earth project. If it maintains its balance, it will be further evidence that we have, in fact, developed a new model that can pave the way to a future of balance for environments across the world.

As we are in the process of developing a new philosophy for environmental change, we hope to enlist those of you acquainted with inter-dimensional communication to assist in bringing this co-creative model to the world. It is hoped that some of you will participate for a series of sessions in order to establish the foundation needed for the earth to build upon. The Awakened Earth movement is *bringing together co-creation with substance* as humanity joins with the unseen in these remarkable partnerships.

Earth's Function

As we are advancing a new protocol that has broad ramifications for the earth, we want to propose that those of you reading this material understand the larger function the Awakened Earth is providing. As the Awakened Earth energies are incorporated into environments throughout the world, there will be changes in the way the earth functions. As the energy accumulates within the body of the planet, the earth will become more resilient and her capacity for light will be increased. As the light increases, the earth will take on the attributes of a star, which will help the earth become the Central Sun for the solar system.

The earth has agreed to serve the cosmos by equipping itself with the light necessary for the changes ahead. Up until now in its evolution, the earth has been the keeper of records for the on-going continuum of life. As the earth adapts to its role as light keeper, it will begin to function as a star. In order to function as the Central Sun, the earth will need to hold more light. Gradually, as the earth accumulates more light, she will be in a position to move into her rightful position in the cosmos.

Whenever the Awakened Earth processes are delivered to an environment, there will be an elevation in light. The light will influence the deliberate course the earth is taking. In keeping with this role, the earth will begin to recognize the light from the Awakened Earth processes and take on new attributes. The light from the Awakened Earth processes contains the elements necessary for the earth to fulfill her role. As the earth moves into her position as the Central Sun, she will take on more and more light, allowing her to become the beacon for the universe.

Now that you have a fuller understanding of the scope of this project, the Masters supporting you hope you will take part in the Awakened Earth project in order to accomplish its greater vision. We are sure those of you who are dedicated to serving the earth will realize the scope of the Awakened Earth project and commit to serving in this endeavor.

In spite of mounting evidence, there seems to be a disconnect in much of humanity's awareness of the current weather extremes and what causes them. Nature, with all of its wisdom, cannot conceive imbalance. It is a body in alignment with balance, and yet, there is imbalance. These imbalances are impacting the earth on a wider and wider scale. In time as these imbalances increase in intensity and frequency, there will be consequences to pay. Nature has the ability to right these imbalances. And so it seems there is but one place to turn; co-creation. With the advent of *The Awakened Earth*, we are in a position to correct many of the imbalances currently visiting the world's stage. In the weeks and months to come, as *The Awakened Earth* emerges from its birthing place, we are hopeful that humanity will come to its senses in sufficient numbers to re-stabilize its many deteriorating environments. Without help, the earth cannot continue its path forward with any degree of certainty. Consider this a wake up call.

CHAPTER 9

Environments Ready for the Awakened Earth

There are many environments suitable for the Awakened Earth. As we have stated before, there are numerous ways the Awakened Earth may be utilized. First and foremost, there are environments throughout the world in need of rebalancing. With the advent of the Awakened Earth Project, we can begin to reestablish the necessary balance for Earth's health. It has been established that once these processes have been utilized, there will be a significant reduction in the imbalances.

Long ago, when this project was conceived, it was hoped that the introduction of balanced energy there would result in a rebalancing to generate health for earth. We now have the proof we were seeking. Furthermore, with the Awakened Earth processes, we have a mechanism that is easy to implement and delivers optimal results.

Once these processes have been implemented, the beneficiary environment will rapidly come into balance. Each environment has its own set of issues to be addressed, yet each environment also impacts the larger biosphere. We have constructed a program to ensure the maximum benefit for the earth. This will require some planning on the part of those of you invested in this project. In the interim, however, we suggest the following primary environments receive the benefit of these Awakened Earth processes.

These environments are primary because they have the ability to greatly impact the overall environment, and because they are in great need. By addressing these environments first, we will be laying a foundation for future projects to build upon. Once these environments have received the Awakened Earth energies, subsequent environments will come into balance more quickly.

The primary environments are:

- The Amazon River Basin
- The tributaries of the Hudson Bay Region
- The coastlines of the Gulf of Mexico
- The wilderness region of Alaska
- The Alaskan/Aleutian Islands
- The region of Vancouver, British Columbia
- The region of Central America, particularly the Nicaraguan Coast
- The Columbian and Brazilian rainforests

Secondary environments to be addressed are:

- The Ethiopian mountain ranges
- The Yangtze and the Huang He Rivers in the Orient
- The mountain ranges in Afghanistan
- The coastlines of Indonesia
- The rivers of Bulgaria

- The region known as the Black Rainforest in Hungary
- The land that borders Pakistan and Iran.
- The Mara River Basin between Kenya and Tanzania

These environments also are in need of immediate attention so that the earth can come into balance more quickly. Once these environments have received the benefit of the Awakened Earth processes, we can begin to address other environments in need of rebalancing.

It is important to launch the Awakened Earth Project with the environments most in need of help, so that the planet can begin the process of coming into balance. Many of you will have environments of your own to address, and we will bring those environments into sustainable balance as well. The important thing to remember is that we are launching a project that will help the planet in its entirety. Our focus will be to bring the Earth into sustainable balance.

There is a need for coordination in the beginning stages so that the earth can benefit from the infusion of these new energies. Our priority is to address those environments most in need. Subsequent to that, we will gladly assist you with other environmental issues. We also will offer our expertise in areas of personal concern such as organizations in need of balance or health-related issues not responding to conventional treatment. Our main obligation is to bring health and balance to natural environments across the globe.

Conditions for Change

The earth has recently been experiencing an influx of harmonious energy, which has helped to elevate consciousness. With this increase has come a readiness to forge a new way of living within the emerging world. The emerging world is defined by a readiness on the part of humanity to step into a co-creative model and utilize its principles.

Some attention has been given to the way in which each condition for change is approached. Many have entertained the idea that the earth is in jeopardy and needs help. While some are aware that the earth can no longer support the needs of humanity, others are still beating the drum for continued misuse of the environment. Of course, this cannot continue without disastrous results. While nature attempts to bring balance, humanity still seeks to destroy it, often in ignorance. While we cannot condone such behavior, we can begin the process of educating.

By conditions for change, we are referring to the manner in which the earth is coming of age in order to fulfill her function in the greater universe. Soon, it will become apparent that the earth has begun to acclimate to higher frequencies that are currently making their way into the Earth's atmosphere. These frequencies have within them a more refined resonance that allows for the earth to be held in a higher resonance. With these higher resonances, the Awakened Earth will provide the impetus for the earth to function in a more sustainable way.

The earth has recognized the energy given to it through the Awakened Earth processes. Primarily, what we are striving for in the Awakened Earth project is for the processes to function in a manner that is consistent with the natural laws. We will be using terms consistent with the way the earth functions naturally. We are introducing an entirely new format for working in a co-creative partnership, but we are introducing methods that are consistent with the natural laws.

This book is a product of extensive research on the part of nature. Nature has the capacity to bring processes into existence that are in alignment with the natural order, and we have done so.

As the Awakened Earth project is a co-creative endeavor, it is also in alignment with the natural laws and will deliver the results we are seeking. This book is the brainchild of several Masters who are committed to raising the vibration of the entire planet. This will elevate the earth as she comes into her new role in the universe. As we are exercising the right to bring this material forward in this time of great transition, we promise a product we deem worthwhile. Never before have we authored such a work on behalf of the greater consciousness.

We look forward to the time when these partnerships are fully functioning and will provide the support necessary for the earth to come into greater balance. Over time, as these partnerships take root, we will be able to bring you changes in protocols that may impact a particular environment. While each environment is different, there are significant similarities present in all environments. Some adjustments may be needed as the partnerships are establishing. We are attempting to bridge the seen and the unseen, using the latest technology to support not only the partnerships, but the Awakened Earth Project as a whole.

Presentations from Earlier Awakened Earth Guidance

To demonstrate the evolution of the Awakened Earth, I am inserting some guidance I received during the time while I was working on this book. I have gotten several related messages from my guidance that illustrate the depth and continuity of thought I was given. These messages illustrate the commitment of the Masters to bring us a functional product.

The following messages supply a timeline that also illustrates the functioning capacity of the co-creative partnership. There have been several different co-creative partnerships to bring this book to fruition.

November 1, 2005
Quan Yin and Gaia

Given the nature of this project, it will be of utmost importance to allow humanity to retake responsibility for the condition of the earth. Otherwise, the results will be disastrous for all humankind. We have spent decades in preparation for the time when humanity would be able to step up and assume its proper role as custodian for the earth. Often, in these intervening years, there have been times when we have wanted to usurp your power and bring balance to the planet—but we were unable to do so, because it would violate the very laws we are seeking to uphold. Now, however, as we have been approached by many of you, we are in a position to help you restore the balance that is sorely needed.

The time has come to present to the world at large the principles of co-creative science. We have begun a new era. With the advent of co-creative science, there is a pathway to recovery. This pathway necessitates trust between humanity and nature. Without this, there would be a breakdown.

We have consistently applied the natural laws to all of our undertakings with humanity. However, until now, humanity did not fully understand the nature of these laws. Furthermore, when humanity reached out to nature, nature did not have the means of communication necessary for a full co-creative partnership. That is no longer so. With the advent of kinesiology as a communication vehicle, we were finally in a position to help humanity recover the custodianship of the planet.

Note: What we did not have at the time was the expanded pendulum response. Kinesiology, or muscle response, was our only means of communication. *Awakened Earth Masters, March 2010.*

November 10, 2005
Metatron and Gaia

To be sure that this information reaches the targeted audience, we are tailoring it for their readership. In this way, we hope to circumvent any comments from the more mainstream audience. This work is for a specific purpose. It is designed to give those of you who are capable of interfacing a way to help the earth immediately. Otherwise, we risk losing valuable ground in our desire to restore balance to many critically impaired environments. It is our hope that once these principles are made available, there will be sufficient numbers to begin the correction process immediately.

February 15, 2006
Metatron

Together with humanity, we will be addressing some of the critical needs for the earth to remain in balance. There will be some new processes to incorporate into the existing processes. In order to simplify the implementation of the processes, we will divide some of the processes into more manageable pieces. This will give those who are coming to this work without prior knowledge the opportunity to work with this format without undue difficulty.

Some of this material will have to be revised to incorporate the two new processes. When this is done, there will be a shift in the overall dynamic of the Awakened Earth project. The shift will strengthen all the processes and give them a cohesive element that is missing at the present time. A more productive process will follow. This will give this work the needed momentum to significantly alter its effectiveness.

February 18, 2006
Metatron

Because of the evolving circumstances with the ongoing weather changes, it is incumbent upon us to address these conditions. To do so, we will be revising some of the earlier material so that it corresponds to the overall, expanded intention. The revised intention incorporates the way in which the earth has been responding to the introduction of these processes over the past two years. Regardless of the conclusions that we have drawn, there seems to be a change in the way the earth is adjusting itself to the influx of these new energies. From what we can tell, the earth is incorporating these new energies in a way that allows for greater balance in the overall revitalization of the affected environments.

In keeping with our desire to achieve greater stability, there is little doubt that these processes have favorably impacted these environments. While we continue to observe the way in which these environments are acclimating to the energies, we will also be watching for any signs of overall improvement.

Together with humanity, we will be initiating some of the newest endeavors ever to bring harmony to areas of neglect and degradation. These endeavors will usher in a wave of energy unlike any that has been utilized for purposes of environmental matters. These energies are compatible with the higher levels of consciousness.

To bring greater balance to the overall earth will be the first priority of our work. The earth has sustained severe exploitation and cannot continue to exist in balance with humanity without substantive help. These processes are designed to help the earth to regain some of her balance. When the time comes to offer this material to those who can assist, we will be ushering in a new era. For the first time, there will be a coordinated effort to responsibly bring balance to the entire earth. Many of you will be participating in a far-reaching and unprecedented event.

Given that we have been in co-creative partnership with some of you for several years, we will be relying on you to take the lead with this far-reaching endeavor. Some of you have been asking for ways to help the earth. The way is now here. It is up to you to decide whether to participate or not.

In keeping with our commitment to help you help the earth, we have brought you this Awakened Earth project. The project itself has given us the opportunity to work extensively with some of you over recent months. This group of dedicated women has come together many times with the hope that the material we have been presenting would eventually benefit mankind. The time has come to acknowledge your efforts and thank you for your diligence. We are at the brink of a new age. This age will be marked as the co-creative age.

March 16, 2006
Gaia

We have undergone several changes as we have sought to deliver this material. This has necessitated that some of the material be reworked. To do this, we are proposing two things.

First, we ask that you consider bringing the Awakened Earth project into alignment with the higher frequencies that have contributed to the formation of the entire project. Second, we ask that you align yourself with these frequencies so that there will be an alignment between yourself and the Awakened Earth project. This is to be done by stating the following: "I request that the Awakened Earth project be aligned with the new energies currently coming into the earth's atmosphere."

The Awakened Earth model has the potential to bring harmony into situations that have never experienced harmony before. Many environments are experiencing severe imbalances, which have caused an entire ecosystem to be in a state of collapse. Until recently, it was thought that little could be done. However, with the onset of this project, there has been significant improvement to the environments that have received the benefit of the Awakened Earth model.

These successes have given impetus to bringing the Awakened Earth project to the public as soon as possible. A decision has been made at the highest levels of the universe to see that this project is expedited by harnessing the power of the new energies. We will be developing a suitable format so that each process will be clear, concise, and uniform. Until we can bring the processes into alignment with the new energies, we will have to rely upon those of you implementing them to be in harmony with these new energies. Some changes to the wording may be needed so that there is consistency throughout all of the processes.

As you can see from these comments from my Awakened Earth guidance, there has been considerable effort to bring this work to you in a form that not only gives you the processes but also allows you to understand some of the background of how this project has evolved over time.

Further Environments for Consideration

In addition to the primary and secondary environments already mentioned, the Awakened Earth project will be in a position to support additional regions. Other environments also need help from the Awakened Earth processes. These environments are scattered throughout the United States. One of the areas in need of treatment is the Panhandle of Texas, which has suffered from the recent drought and needs to be brought into alignment with the surrounding ecosystem.

The next environment for your consideration is in the Colorado Plateau, where there has been significant loss of habitat due to extensive development. We also would like you to consider the region known as "the corn belt." This region is subject to severe flooding and will lose its vitality if it does not receive help soon.

There are many other environments that can be helped by utilizing the Awakened Earth model. There are several zones that have been inundated with pervasive flooding. In particular need are the areas impacted along the Red River in North and South Dakota, as well as the Iowa River. These areas have undergone rapid deterioration in soil quality and injuries to the ecosystem.

The purpose of this model is to demonstrate the value of co-creative science to bring balance to great areas of neglect and exploitation. Once these processes are known as effective ways to rejuvenate a wide array of environments, we are confident the exploitation and neglect can be mitigated and even reversed. As we take this project to the world, let us be mindful that we are broadening the scope of co-creation. It has unlimited potential. As we embark on this fascinating journey, we are mindful of the significance of this endeavor to radically change not only consciousness, but the way nature itself is viewed. You have before you solutions to major environmental dilemmas.

Current Example of an Environmental Project: The Hurricane Corridor

Let me say here that sometimes the Awakened Earth Masters will tell you beforehand how many sessions a particular environment will take. Other times, they may not know. Sometimes it will be apparent that the number of sessions can be measured by the amount of neglect an environment has endured. A severely damaged environment will understandably require more sessions than an environment whose main issue is rebalancing. The following worksheets will demonstrate how this project began. They are taken directly from my notes as I endeavored to bring balance to the Hurricane Corridor. In total, there were fifteen sessions.

Environmental Project Worksheet

Date: 6-23-09

Session: #1

Follow-up date: 7-1-09

Project: Hurricane Corridor   *Amount of Light:* 6

Project location: Atlantic Ocean, running from the East Coast of Africa through the Caribbean Sea and into the Gulf of Mexico

Intention: To create an environment that reduces the likelihood for severe storms to develop.

Co-creative partners present: Awakened Earth Masters, Gaia, Deva of Atlantic Ocean, Deva of the Caribbean and Deva of the Gulf of Mexico

Indicated number of sessions: 15

Processes: # 7   The Harmony Process

Duration: 6 minutes

Partnership message: As you settle into your heart space, remember the wisdom awaiting you. As you witness these waters, you are calling forth an aggregate from the body of nature who can deliver the necessary components for fulfillment of this intention. As you observe the waters, you are accepting a co-creative role in bringing to this environment the constructive elements required for its fulfillment. This will enable this environment to come into balance.

Environmental Project Worksheet

Date: 7-1-09

Session: # 2

Follow-up date: 7-7-09

Project: Hurricane Corridor　　　　　　*Amount of Light:* 6

Co-creative partners present: Awakened Earth Masters, Deva of Atlantic Ocean, Deva of the Caribbean, Deva of the Gulf of Mexico, and Overlighting Deva for Earth

Processes: # 15　　Dynamic of Harmony and Well-being

Duration: Two minutes

The Overlighting Deva for Earth was called in to lend its energy in support of this endeavor. Its energy is equivalent to several dynamics and offers greater cohesion as we bring balance to these waters. The Overlighting Deva for Earth is a resource beyond any other.

Environmental Project Worksheet

Date: 7-7-09
Session: #3
Follow-up Date: 7-13-09

Project: Hurricane Corridor

Description of Environment: (Same as session # 1)

Intention: To create an environment that reduces the likelihood for severe storms to develop

Co-Creative Partners Present: Awakened Earth Masters, Overlighting Deva for Earth

Processes: # 15   Dynamic of Harmony and Well-being

Duration: Two minutes

As the hurricane season comes to a close, it is worth noting that there were no severe storms that hit the United States mainland in 2009. While there have been minor disturbances and tropical systems, there have not been hurricanes. The reason is clear. The Awakened Earth processes were delivered in a timely and proficient manner, giving the entire Hurricane Corridor the energy and elements necessary for the environment to come into a stable state of being.

The Awakened Earth model delivered a resoundingly successful set of processes to the entire hurricane field. In doing so, we prevented severe storms from developing. This success has saved billions of dollars by preventing disaster. Furthermore, it has given the environments the necessary elements to withstand future devastation. This has more than exemplified the quality and power of the Awakened Earth.

CHAPTER 10

The Scope of Environmentalism

As we are introducing a model for bringing environments into balance, we want to develop programs that can further the causes of environmentalism. Environmentalism, in our view, is the most misunderstood concept of the twenty-first century.

Environmentalists have, by their nature, often offended the establishment. Much of the misunderstanding stems from the environmentalist's inability to recognize the scope of environmentalism. It has been said that an environmentalist is someone who cannot separate the forest from the trees. We would have to agree. By their nature, environmentalists are savvy individuals who sometimes cannot lift their view to see the larger picture. They focus on individual issues rather than on the whole.

Because of this approach, they understand less than the whole. Take, for example, the environmentalists who want to protect an individual species without considering the effects on the entire natural world. An individual species, while worthwhile, is not important enough to warrant saving if the larger environment suffers.

We are proposing a view of the environment that considers all life valuable, yet recognizes that there are times when, for the betterment of the whole, a species needs to be sacrificed. The conditions for determining when a species is in jeopardy and needs to be saved vary considerably. In the case of the salmon spawning in the rivers of Idaho, there are significant reasons to save the species, even though they are contributing to the demise of the inland tributaries as they spawn further and further upstream. This habit of salmon has raised concerns over the welfare of the inland habitat and has made the state unable to determine the fate of its tributaries.

When environmentalists enter the picture, there are heated debates over which has more value, the salmon or the tributaries. No one actually knows, because no one has the larger perspective. But nature does. With the Awakened Earth Project, nature can be consulted. Nature always has the larger view and considers the most effective means, as well as the most advantageous solutions, for all life.

Using co-creation, the implementation of the most suitable means will be handled by the Awakened Earth Masters—in partnership with humanity—on an environment-by-environment basis. There will no longer be a need for the human partner to ascertain the most suitable means for any given environment, because the co-creative partnership will do so.

In the future, there will be other new measures to balance environments. When the time comes, we will bring them to you. We wanted you to be aware of these future measures. As the

Awakened Earth processes take root, there will be times when the Awakened Earth Masters will introduce the new measures. We will do so on the Awakened Earth website. These measures will begin to function in a balanced manner, which will support the earth as it continues its journey into the light.

Global Warming as Viewed by Nature

There are significant schools of thought regarding the phenomenon known as global warming. With the collapse of the Arctic Ice Shelf comes the warning that the earth is in danger. Much has been written of the importance of this monumental collapse. From our viewpoint, this collapse signals the beginning of an era of common need. The need is magnified by how humanity interprets this calamity.

In the annals of earth's history, there has never been an era of enlightenment such as the one the Earth is experiencing today. The earth has, by agreement, come to a point in her history that will allow her to move into a greater harmony with the larger universe. The collapse of the ice shelf has come about because of factors beyond human understanding. First of all, there have been significant shifts in the plates beneath the ice shelf.

The common link between these shifts and the ice shelf is the gravitational pull created by the passage of longstanding cycles in the Earth's continuum. As these cycles have endured for millions of years, there has not been a need for measurements. In addition to human endeavors, which have had an impact on the acceleration of the melting of the Arctic regions, there are current indicators of the rapid melting that have gone unnoticed. In other words, there are subjective reasons for the earth's current state.

The environment, however, does warrant concern and even alarm. Global warming has caused an awakening in the human consciousness. There has also been an imperative to adjust the way humanity views its relationship with the earth itself. As more and more people are learning about humanity's impact on its environment, there is hope that the spread of this awareness will bring about a change in thinking.

Global warming is, in part, the result of human endeavors. However, with the advent of The Awakened Earth project, the earth has the opportunity to align itself with balance. This balance will correct much of the uncertainty regarding the future of the planet. Earth has the ability to come into balance. As the results of the Awakened Earth processes are observed, there is likely to be a push to alleviate some of the environmental stresses brought about by human endeavor.

Because the Earth has sustained great harm and is in danger of falling into severe imbalance, we have developed measures to equip humanity to bring about major re-balancing, so that the earth and humanity can continue on this journey of life together. In an endeavor to correct the imbalances, we have initiated The Awakened Earth model to give humanity the opportunity to reverse the damage that has been done. We, of nature and beyond, are hopeful that, together with humanity, we can begin a revitalization project unlike any undertaken before.

At this point in the evolutionary cycle, there is an opportunity for the inhabitants of earth to be made mindful of their inextricable link to the earth as a living organism. Earth has the inherent capacity to balance itself, using its own resources. However, without the intervention of the Awakened Earth processes, the continuation of earth and humanity living together will be in jeopardy.

The Awakened Earth model will give the earth and humanity an opportunity to evolve, using co-creative means. Earth is at a turning point. She can work co-creatively with humanity for the betterment of all, insuring the continuation with humanity. Or we can see the alternative, in which the earth would continue without humanity.

There are means, other than the Awakened Earth, already in motion that will help to bring stability to the earth. This model contends that humanity, working in partnership with nature and the Awakened Earth Masters, can alleviate the current stresses and give the earth the support necessary to allow both the planet and humanity to evolve together.

The Internet as Support

The Awakened Earth website is in development and will be operational in 2010. The site will serve as a means for the Awakened Earth Project to function globally and also be supportive locally. Awakened Earth.com will bring the partnerships a place to convene and will provide a forum for new information as well as a place to share issues and concerns.

As the development continues, the website will become the central location for the partnerships to interact, ask questions, and receive updates and relevant information. Because this entire project is new, there will be details to work out. In this dynamic process, which will be a worldwide endeavor, the website will be useful as a means for the partnerships to interact and to receive information in a timely manner. Over time, as these partnerships take root, we will be able to bring you up-to-date information that will broaden our capacity to help many partnerships. While each environment is different, there are significant similarities present in all environments that will make sharing information among groups beneficial.

To make the Awakened Earth website useful, the groups will need to contribute information. As we bring more and more partnerships on board, we will need a method for the partnerships to interchange information and help one another in maintaining their environments satisfactorily. The site will include a place to post successes, which will give other partnerships the ability to view these individual successes and apply the circumstances, when applicable, to their own environments. The achievements of the Awakened Earth can be magnified by sharing, via the website, the exact nature of how an environment was treated.

We are establishing a forum for partnerships to interact on the website. We foresee a time when partnerships will be able to directly converse with each other. The technology is available, and we will utilize it as soon as we can, because much of what we are contemplating will come as the result of the partnerships sharing their information. As soon as we are able, we will broaden the capacity of the Awakened Earth website to meet the growing needs of the project. We will encourage the partnerships to identify their projects and post their results so that we can formulate a way to maximize the effectiveness of the internet.

The Awakened Earth website will give us a way to update you with information gathered from the partnerships. This information will provide substance for discussion, using examples directly from the partnerships. Also, the data that is shared from the partnerships will begin to demonstrate the variety of situations that can receive the benefit from the Awakened Earth processes. The website also will provide a central location for all matters that pertain to the Awakened Earth project.

The website will create opportunities for some individuals, who will work with the partnerships in establishing expedient means for posting their information. We are hopeful that someone familiar with co-creative partnerships will want to help expand the website, utilizing the latest technologies. The evidence gathered in the field can be placed on the website and utilized for maximum effectiveness. Some of you may consider helping with this aspect of the site. Because we are introducing a project whose scope is not yet determined, we need to develop a format that is responsive to the growing needs of the partnerships.

We will continue to be cognizant of the emerging needs of the participants. We hope to deliver a website capable of addressing those needs in a manner that is superlative and filled with useful material. There may be communication challenges in a project of this scope, but we believe there also will be solutions. In time, the website will deliver what is needed and will do so in a manner that supports the partnerships and the Awakened Earth Project. As we equip the partnerships to care for the environment, we want the website to care for you.

The Awakened Earth Masters plan to be involved with the website. We will offer timely information that is relevant to the functioning of the earth, including answers to questions posted to the website by the partnerships. In this way, we hope to be interactive with the partnerships. The author has agreed to function as an intermediary for us so that you, the reader, will have access to the very latest information.

CHAPTER 11

States That Have Been Helped

Several environments already have benefited from the energies presented by the Awakened Earth Project. It was through these environments that we first took note of the impact these energies might have. It became apparent that, once the processes were implemented, the environments began to respond favorably.

The following states have been the recipient of the Awakened Earth energies. Each has begun to rebalance in a way that is consistent with the natural order. Each environment was supplied with an intention. Significantly, each intention represented the underlying issue causing the imbalance. In the case of Florida, the major issue causing imbalance was the fragile coastline. As the Awakened Earth processes were introduced, the coastlines began to adapt to the energies by coming into a more harmonious balance. No matter what intention was stated, there was a consistency in each environment enabling it to come into a more refined state of balance.

Florida

In the beginning, when the Awakened Earth was in its formative stages, it was thought unlikely that Florida could receive substantial help. But it soon became clear that the Awakened Earth processes were distinctly different and were delivering energetic components capable of re-establishing balance and providing health. Gradually, it was understood that many Florida environments were taking on new attributes, which were not only balanced but also bringing a new measure of light. This success gave rise to a new way of addressing not only environments, but the earth itself.

No one could have been more surprised than we were. The extraordinary results were noticeably consistent. New vegetation began showing up along the coastlines of Florida, which helped the coastline to rejuvenate and stabilize in ways we had not seen before. We concluded that, once the coastlines were prepared through the Awakened Earth methods, there was a substantial lessening of the imbalances that had been in place for so long. The grasses and other vegetation were coming into a new state of harmony, which could be attributed to nothing else but the Awakened Earth methodology.

When we observed the overall balance along the Gulf Coast, we were pleasantly surprised to see it was holding up as well. This gave us the impetus to further our research as to why this was happening. During this time, the author was attempting to give Florida extra care, using the Awakened Earth processes in place at the time. The combination of consistent application of the Awakened Earth measures and the subsequent additions of more processes gave Florida the "juice" it needed to reverse decades of abuse. As time went on, it was apparent that these processes were helping to create a new balance.

California

In California, the situation we were facing had more to do with drought than anything else. The initial stages of the Awakened Earth were underway, so we decided to apply the newly formed processes to addressing the extreme drought conditions.

As this was done, two things occurred. First of all, there was a lessening of on-going drought in the San Diego area. Secondly, there was a buildup in the reservoirs over much of San Diego County. This endeavor proved to be fruitful enough to convince us that some remarkable changes were, in fact, occurring.

We began to see other improvements in the overall balance of the larger ecosystem. We expected the reservoirs to lose their water as the season progressed; they did not. This gave us the evidence we were looking for. Once the Awakened Earth processes have been introduced, the entire ecosystem tends to maintain its balance.

Initially, we thought there would be some components of the environment that would need further assistance in order to maintain balance. But they did not. We have learned that when the Awakened Earth processes are employed, greater sustainability occurs. We have observed this many times.

It also came as a surprise to us that, once the Awakened Earth Processes had been injected into an environment, the entire ecosystem came into greater harmony. Harmony is the prerequisite for balance, so the initial offerings of the Awakened Earth set the stage for further balance by first incorporating harmony. This was evidenced by the way in which several of the fire-prone areas were no longer subject to imbalances, which often set the stage for fires. It was clear to us that the ecosystem at large was incorporating a new balance, enabling the area to resist fire. In the years since these processes were first initiated, San Diego County has experienced fewer devastating fires than in the years before the Awakened Earth processes began.

The California Firefighters Association did not have adequate firefighting equipment to deal with the 2007 San Diego firestorm. Once the fires were in progress, this hazard caused a ripple effect throughout San Diego County. The environment was unable to hold back the massive amount of wind and fire, which made the fire spread and move across the county without restriction. If the Awakened Earth processes had been utilized, with an intention to minimize fire danger, the results could have been less severe.

We have witnessed that a treated environment can alter its behavior, once the energy in these new and sustaining processes are in place. Soon, it will be possible to protect an environment, once the Awakened Earth Model has been introduced. The Awakened Earth has the components to bring an environment into balance and give it the protection to withstand ongoing weather-related disruptions.

What this means for the future remains to be seen and will depend upon the amount of support the Awakened Earth project receives. It also will depend on the willingness of those of you committed to the earth to shepherd this project through the next decade. Humanity and nature can work together for the betterment of all life. What we have seen leads us to believe this is entirely possible. As more people are made aware of the existence of this co-creative means to deliver balance to the earth, we feel certain more of them will find that the answers they seek lie in the pages of this book. Never before have we made such a proclamation.

With the advent of the Awakened Earth model, we have begun to witness changes in the way an environment responds after the processes have been delivered. Major areas of farmland in California are subject to infestation from non-indigenous vegetation as the result of increasingly high temperatures. Conditions in California's fertile valleys need a boost from the Awakened Earth processes so that they can rejuvenate and begin to produce the kind of food necessary for health.

The condition of these valleys is becoming serious enough to warrant full-fledged partnerships dedicated to correcting the imbalances they are currently experiencing. These valleys are crucial to maintaining a consistent environment for the growing of food.

South Carolina

Recently, South Carolina was experiencing an extreme drought, particularly in the upstate region. This region had begun to dry up in a manner that was causing alarm. The reservoirs were down as much as twenty feet. In addition, farmland was being dried up in an unprecedented manner. Farmers had to purchase supplemental feed for livestock, paying exorbitant prices, as hay was no longer available in adequate measure. This situation caused some farmers to liquidate their livestock in favor of farming crops, which were less rain dependent. Others opted out of farming altogether—a move that was potentially hazardous to the local economy.

As recently as April of 2009, farmers have been concerned with local rainfall. However, the Awakened Earth processes have been applied with diligence, over recent months, giving South Carolina the rainfall it has sorely needed. With ongoing monitoring, we believe there is no reason this drought should continue.

North Carolina

In the case of North Carolina, there has been a remarkable shift in the amount of rain. In the early spring of 2009, the western North Carolina mountains were experiencing rainfall totals averaging six inches less than normal. These deficits were reduced significantly in April and May.

The entire ecosystem in that area is experiencing new balance as a direct result of Awakened Earth processes. We expect the changes in this ecosystem to magnify the balance and, therefore, allow the region to come into even greater harmony than previously thought possible. Crops have been yielding significantly more food than they had in recent years, and we expect this trend to continue. Food supplies will be enhanced by the application of the Awakened Earth processes. Because we are facing new challenges with food supplies, it is of particular interest to us that the Awakened Earth processes be introduced into environments so that all aspects of the environment flourish.

As North Carolina comes into greater balance, there are certain to be those who will realize a great movement is underway. There has been an effort to explain the recent rainfall in terms that are no longer suitable. As the new paradigm unfolds, there will need to be greater understanding of the forces underlying the changes in environments that have been treated with the Awakened Earth processes. As the world comes to a greater understanding of the forces beyond measure, it will be important to demonstrate the value in the Awakened Earth model of co-creation. This can be done by giving examples of the major environments that already have benefited from Awakened Earth energies.

After these processes were focused on the western North Carolina mountains, instead of drought and heat, those areas experienced a return to a more natural balance. In the short term, this environment has begun to approximate earlier times when there was little human interference and the earth was capable of remaining sustainable. Over time, as these processes continue to be introduced into this mountain environment, there will be greater and greater stability. As the environment comes into this more refined state, there will be much greater balance than ever before. Slowly, often by imperceptible increments, the environment will become stronger and more capable of maintaining its balance, because of improvement in the overall ecosystem.

The western North Carolina mountains have continued to receive the benefit of the Awakened Earth processes. However, there have been some difficulties in bringing about an ongoing moisture balance. Some of that is attributable to the greater environment that expands beyond these mountains.

A series of unusual developments have given rise to unstable conditions throughout the southeast, including a high number of disturbances along the western portions of the Appalachians. These disturbances have pulled moisture away from the mountain tops and into the lower portions of the south, creating near-record rainfall in parts of Florida. Additionally, there has been insufficient rain in other areas of the country. These drought-stricken areas, such as Texas, also have contributed to the overall conditions in the southeast.

We have witnessed the environment of the mountains in North Carolina coming into balance while the surrounding environments experienced weather extremes. It stands to reason that, once these other environments receive help from the Awakened Earth Project, there will be a greater balance in larger ecosystems and this will contribute to the health and balance of greater portions of the United States.

Once the Awakened Earth Project is introduced into several environments throughout the United States, there will come a time when the larger ecosystem will come into greater balance as well. While there is much to be gained from addressing smaller environments, such as the western North Carolina mountains, there will be an even greater impact once the larger ecosystem has been addressed. Until then, imbalances will continue to be a problem for smaller environments.

With these and other examples, as mentioned in this book, we are confident in predicting a satisfactory future for treated environments throughout the world. It is also apparent that once these processes have been introduced, the entire environment takes on a quality of balance not present before.

In some badly troubled areas, we are in a race against time. We hope to begin implementing these magnificent energetic infusions to environments across the globe soon.

So far, the 2010 season is much wetter than previous seasons. While this is good news, it is not an indicator that the season will continue to be wet without on-going applications of the Awakened Earth processes. However, the improvements resulting from the Awakened Earth applications in 2009 are impressive. In western North Carolina alone the fire danger has been reduced by nearly seventy percent over 2008. While this is dramatic and demonstrates the capacity for significant impact to the environment, it also is a reminder that on-going stability requires on-going Awakened Earth applications to continue to allow the environment to remain in balance. In specific terms, the western North Carolina region has benefitted considerably as a result of the water tables filling and becoming more stable. The local *Asheville Citizen-Times* reported on March 29, 2010 the following:

591 acres burned in 2009, with 62.13 inches of rain

2,058 acres burned in 2008, with 35.63 inches of rain

2654 acres burned in 2007, with 34.39 inches of rain

From our perspective, the Awakened Earth processes have contributed to this reduction in acres burned and increase in rainfall.

South Dakota

In the spring of 2009, there was rampant flooding along the Red River, which caused extremely high waters. These waters were in danger of spilling over the banks of the Red River. However, with the introduction of the Awakened Earth processes, these floodwaters were mitigated. Furthermore, future flooding was prevented. Editor's note: In 1997 the Red River valley experienced catastrophic flooding that caused more than $3.5 billion in destruction.

Without exception, whenever the Awakened Earth processes are introduced into an environment, balance is restored. In South Dakota, there were several incidents when flooding was imminent but did not occur. The power of these processes cannot be understated. They have no equal.

Pacific Northwest (WA, OR, ID)

The Awakened Earth processes have been introduced into the Pacific Northwest. The designated purpose was "to bring balance to the weather patterns causing excessive drought and high temperatures." This area suffered from some of the highest temperatures and extended drought in recent memory. The Pacific Northwest also has suffered the loss of large portions of forest as the result of excess timber harvesting, which has weakened the balance of the entire ecosystem by causing severe trauma to the natural habitat. All living matter in the ecosystem was experiencing ongoing hardship.

Without intervention from the Awakened Earth model for restoration, this ecosystem would not be able to stay in balance or adjust to the ravages perpetuated by severe timber harvesting. When we began this restoration, it was evident that bringing the area into full balance would require many months of deliberate Awakened Earth applications. We asked the author to forego these applications in favor of finishing the book you are now reading, so that many would have the benefit of these remarkable energies.

In order to establish ongoing balance to the Pacific Northwest, the Awakened Earth energies will have to be supplied to this environment for at least six months. The first of the processes was introduced in July of 2009. While it will be some time before the results are noticeable, the environment will become more stabilized. To ease the environment into balance will be the first goal of the Awakened Earth. It is hoped that someone will take on this project as soon as this book is published.

The Hurricane Corridor

The Hurricane Corridor was our first attempt to bring balance to a large swath of an environment, to facilitate balance while, at the same time, preventing mass destruction of habitat. This project has far surpassed anything we could have imagined. There were no hurricanes to hit the United States mainland the summer that we began using these processes. Contrary to news accounts that El Nino was the force behind the quiet hurricane season, it was, in fact, because the Awakened Earth processes had been delivered into this hurricane field.

The environment remained stabilized throughout the fall of 2009, even though no additional processes were delivered after August 30, 2009. What this tells us is that environments that have received the benefit of the Awakened Earth processes will remain in balance for many months to come. Although we are in the beginning stages of launching this project worldwide, evidence such as this suggests that the power of the Awakened Earth processes continue long after the processes themselves stop.

Many of you reading this material are in a position to help. We know that. Furthermore, we are depending upon those of you whose consciousness is aware to come to this work in order for the earth to function in a more balanced state. The answers are here. Help is available. Will you preserve the earth and the life it offers? Nature and the Awakened Earth Masters are standing by to help you. The capacity for balance is in your hands. We are fervently awaiting your decision.

It is with great honor that we bring the remarkable Awakened Earth model to the earth in these times of great need.

Acknowledgments

It goes without saying that this work would not have been possible without the unconditional support from persons I have met along the way. Many have contributed their expertise and given me encouragement when I had little faith in my ability to fulfill my ambition. Others have stood by me and helped me clarify what I hoped to achieve. As I began to realize the scope of this endeavor, I purposely committed to seeing it through. I held firmly to the belief that the Awakened Earth could become a reality.

Without the help of the following persons, I dare say the Awakened Earth would not be. In acknowledgment I wish to first thank my husband, Jim, for giving me the freedom to work on this project for several years. His steadfast support has encouraged me and given me strength when my own strength was faltering. Others who have contributed their expertise are Jan Tober, who knew from the outset that this work had promise. She has earned her stars for giving me the belief that the Awakened Earth was a valid model for blessing the planet. In addition to Jan, this work would not be possible without the efforts of Ellen Kaufman Dosick and Karen Wolfer, who freely contributed their expertise in pursuit of helping the earth. Together, these three women helped me bring the Awakened Earth into this time-space continuum.

I wish to thank Sandi Tomlin-Sutker for her initial editing help. She guided me into the process of editing and gave me confidence with the overall business of editing. Additional editing help was provided by Pamela Guerrieri, whose excellence in all facets of the editing process gave me comfort and confidence. She also thoroughly guided me through the production proofing with ease and equanimity. The overall production management was superbly guided by Ellen Reid, my astute and creative book shepherd. Her efforts produced a worthy team to oversee the process of publishing a book. This work would not have happened without the efforts of my unseen partners: the Awakened Earth Masters, who have unfailingly supported me, the devas, and other unseen forces who have lightened my load and provided me with hours of pleasure. And lastly, to Lee Harris, who opened my heart to the presence of the nature kingdoms way back when.

Appendices

APPENDIX A

Definitions

Balance is the natural state of an environment and is a prerequisite for an environment to come into health.

Consciousness is the relative state of the collective awareness at any given point in time.

Co-creative partnership allows for humanity to form a partnership with the unseen collective referred to as "nature" and with Ascended Masters who are overseers for the earth. The unseen will automatically form a partnership when an intention is invoked.

Crystalline structure creates the bond between all matter. This structure is inherent in all matter.

Deva is a representative of nature and is capable of communicating its intelligence.

Gaia is an interface between the earth and humanity, whose purpose is bringing understanding to humanity's issues and concerns. Gaia's main function is to support humanity in these times of great change.

Intention is the launching pad for humanity to join with nature to implement a co-creative partnership. Intention is a deliberate thought and/or statement of will and the designation of a preferred outcome.

Light is the quotient of available source energy existing at any given moment in time. Light contributes to the overall well-being of any given environment.

Natural order is the essential working structure of the universe.

Nature refers to all non-human living things on the planet and their environment. Nature, for our purposes, is the body of intelligence ready and available to support the Awakened Earth project in its quest for balance and health of earth's environments.

Overlighting deva of earth is a being representative of the nature kingdoms that can bring balance to any of earth's habitats, provided that humanity has called upon her to do so.

Planetary Logos oversees all concerns regarding how the earth functions.

Project is an environment receiving the benefit of the Awakened Earth energies.

Sacred geometry is the architecture for the universe. It is the structure present in all living matter. It gives definition to all living matter and is present in every cell of living matter. The symbols that are used with certain processes are examples of sacred geometry.

Source is broadly defined as the light of all existence and refers to the creating force of the universe.

Source energy is the continuing flow of creative energy through the universe. This energy is the mechanism that allows for all Awakened Earth processes to be implemented. Source energy has the ability to bring balance into any environment with the focus and direction of Awakened Earth measures.

APPENDIX B

Further Explanations for the Awakened Earth

These explanations are for use with the Awakened Earth. They help to illustrate the complexity and depth of the undertaking of this project. These explanations are an illustration of the way in which the Awakened Earth has united varying forces to equip the planet to come into balance.

Alignment

When we use the term alignment, we are referring to the condition of balance and harmony moving in conjunction with a greater purpose. Alignment is the condition that brings balance and harmony into an environment for the purpose of fulfilling an intention. When alignment exists, there is also harmony and balance. Alignment incorporates the condition of balance and harmony by employing universal principles to the stated intention.

Awakened Earth Masters

The Awakened Earth Masters are the backbone of this endeavor. They are intelligent beings that hold the coordinates

necessary for the Awakened Earth to function while simultane-
ously bringing their wisdom to each Awakened Earth partnership.
Each Master has qualities necessary for the earth to become a
fully functioning planet capable of enduring great change. An
Ascended Master is a being that has been designated by God as
a representative of the angel hierarchy.

Balance

Balance is the inherent quality in nature. Nature brings
balance to any situation in need of balance because nature operates *only* from a state of balance. Balance is the state of being
required for an environment to become strengthened. Balance is
incorporated by engaging nature in every co-creative partnership;
engaging a co-creative partnership will automatically establish a
framework for balance. Balance has within it the corresponding
elements required for any environment to be elevated into a state
of balance. Setting an intention also calls upon additional factors
that can deliver balance.

A state of balance is the condition necessary for any environment to be considered healthy. By stating an intention to the
partnership, further balance is introduced into the framework
of the partnership. Bringing an intention to the partnership sets
into motion irrefutable laws that govern all aspects of the Awakened Earth project. The stated intention establishes a working
environment that becomes aligned with the natural laws present
in all of the natural order.

As this work will demonstrate, the environment called into
existence is in balance with the operating forces in the universe.
The fact that balance is incorporated into the formation of each

partnership guarantees that all work that proceeds from each partnership also will be in balance. It can be no other way.

Co-Creative Partnership

For our purposes, a co-creative partnership is a partnership between humanity and members of both nature and the Awakened Earth Masters. The partnership is formed by calling forth nature to assist with the fulfillment of an intention brought to the partnership by humanity. The partnership is then established to deliver the necessary ingredients to fulfill the stated intention. It is not necessary to call forth individual members; they are drawn by the intention and will automatically come to the partnership. The partnership utilizes the ingredients to fulfill the intention supplied by humanity.

Dynamic

A dynamic, for our purposes, is the quality or state of being experienced in the Awakened Earth model for co-creation. It is qualitatively different from other dynamics in that it is aligned with the higher vibrations of the universe. The dynamic present in all Awakened Earth endeavors is aligned with the frequency of harmony.

Energy

Energy, in this context, is the element that exists throughout the universe. Energy has the ability to move from one location to another, and can be moved through intention assisted by a co-creative partnership. The partnership conducts the energy from one location to another based upon the needs of an environment. When energy is moved by direct application for the purpose of improving the health of an environment, there will be an immediate transfer of energy. Energy is equipped to function in a variety of capacities as long as an intention has been set forth. The intention sets the stage for energy to be relocated.

Geometric Designs

In keeping with the overall intention for the Awakened Earth, the need for stabilizing forces is apparent. The elements required for a coordinated environment can be introduced simply by calling upon the insertion of a particular geometric design. With this insertion comes the balance necessary for the environment to be made stable. The geometric design offers a framework for an individual environment to receive the necessary support to bring it into a more balanced state. The design holds the blueprint for the environment to be calibrated to a higher vibration. The end result is an environment that has the stability necessary to come into greater health.

Harmony

Harmony is the state or quality present when a partnership demonstrates its intent to serve the higher good. Harmony is the precursor to balance and remains a component of a balanced partnership. Harmony gives the partnership a measure of influence that supports the overall intention. Once a co-creative partnership has been engaged, forces form to bring a balanced and harmonious state to not only the partnership, but to all work flowing from the partnership. It is as if the partnership taps into the universal pool of harmony and brings it into the intention and, therefore, into the work that flows forth from the intention.

Light

Light is the dominant characteristic of an environment. It is a component made up of several factors. First, light holds elements of resonance, meaning that light is a conductor of energy while, at the same time, distributing energy. Second, light provides the backdrop for an environment to align with its higher nature. And third, light can emerge through the greater consciousness in a manner consistent with the laws of the universe. For these reasons, light is designated as the holder of the blueprint for a higher resonance to emerge. Light has the ability to correct imbalances and to bring the necessary balance to allow for an intention to be fulfilled. Light is an essential force for life and contributes itself without contemplation. Light exists without provocation or stimulation and is present without thought. Light has no objective or reason to be anything other than Light. It serves its purpose as it is dispensed with intention.

The Natural World

Within the Awakened Earth project, we refer to the natural world as the life force that is nature. Nature consists of both seen and unseen bodies. The unseen portion of nature directs itself, within the framework of a co-creative partnership, to deliver balance. Nature has the capacity to bring balance to any situation or environment for the purpose of bringing health. The pursuit of health undergirds all that the Awakened Earth stands for. Co-creative partnerships have the benefit of a balanced force of energy. The natural world lives in a state of balance until humanity intervenes and disrupts the natural order, causing imbalance. The Awakened Earth model includes the mechanisms to bring balance to many diverse situations.

Nature

In the manifest world, you experience nature by perception through your senses. However, much of nature resides in the unseen. The body of nature has an intelligence that can communicate when an intentional partnership is formed for the purpose of administering balance and more. For the Awakened Earth project we, of nature, have been engaged in a co-creative partnership with the author for the purpose of bringing this book to you. In addition, we have engaged Masters who are working on behalf of humanity to serve the greater good. Nature, in this context, is a composite of intelligences that have agreed to serve the greater good.

Resonance

Resonance is a quality or condition needed for an environment to be considered in balance. Resonance can be qualified by its ability to come into vibrational alignment with the other existing elements in any given environment. Resonance also is inherent in the working of a co-creative partnership because resonance offers a vibration compatible with balance. Resonance, while not commonly understood, is a vibrational component necessary for an environment to achieve balance. Resonance has the capacity to ensure stability throughout an environment.

Universal Laws

Universal laws are the unchanging laws or principles that govern all aspects of the universe. Universal laws undergird the natural order of the universe. These laws run through all that is in existence. As you come to nature for the purpose of engaging a co-creative partnership, you will be working within the framework of universal law. Universal laws are the foundation of the universe. They serve to insure stability and help to assure a natural working order. We have utilized several universal laws throughout the Awakened Earth project.

APPENDIX C

Opening and Closing a Session with Nature

To begin an environmental project, follow the steps outlined below. The steps offer substantive guidelines to help you formulate how to work with your partners in nature.

1. Begin by centering within your own being. For our purposes, we will refer to your center as the heart. Spend a few moments bringing yourself into alignment with the greater you.

2. State the intention. The intention alerts the greater body of nature that, along with the Awakened Earth Masters, will assist you in fulfilling the stated intention. *Determining an intention is primary in establishing the partnership's direction.* The intention serves as the blueprint for the co-creative partnership. The Masters have the ability to bring together the exact members to fulfill any stated intention. It is important that the intention complies with the natural order. For example, when you state that you wish to bring rainfall into a particular environment,

we will align ourselves to that particular environment so that the fulfillment of the intention will be in accord with the natural order. Intentions are to be specific so that the unseen will know the precise environment you are working with. The precise location of the environment is necessary so that your partners can fulfill your intention.

3. Take out The Awakened Earth Processes Checklist. Using your pendulum, identify, with your partners, which of the processes are needed to address the stated intention. Usually the processes are implemented in numeric order.

4. Determine the amount of light present by asking your partnership. Note it on your Project Worksheet. The light quotient will be necessary for use with some of the processes, but not all of them.

5. Implement the processes with your partners. Verify that they have been completed.

6. Again using your pendulum, check with your partners for follow-up information. If a follow-up session is indicated, note the follow-up session date on your worksheet. *(I have found that noting the follow-up sessions on a calendar helps me to keep track of environmental sessions and follow-ups.)*

7. To close the session, simply say to your partners, "Thank you, we close for now in the honor of oneness."

APPENDIX D

Expanded Pendulum Responses

These responses are the result of collaboration with nature to ensure more definitive communication. They have eased the burden of understanding so that communication with the unseen has been elevated to a new level. Refer to page 72 for more detailed information.

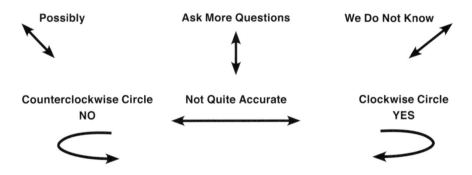

Awakened Earth Processes Checklist

1. Preparing the Environment_____

2. The Collaboration Process_____

3. Color Balance_____Calibration
   Duration: Thirty seconds to four minutes_____
   Infusion Duration: Twenty to sixty seconds_____
                        (The color used will always be red.)

4. Color Attunement_____
   Red, Green, & Gold_____ or Violet_____

5. Attunement with Earth's Vibration_____
   Red, Green, & Gold_____ or Violet_____
   Device Needed: A Chromatic Pitch Instrument or Pitch Pipe

6. Infusion of New Energy_____
   Duration: Two to four minutes_____

7. The Harmony Process_____
   Duration: One to six minutes_____
   * May Include Process # 15_____

8. **Exchange of Energy Process**_____
    Instantaneous transfer

9. **Total Environment Balance**_____
    Balance: Two to six minutes_____
    Stabilization: Fifteen seconds
    * May Include Process # 15_____

10. **The Calibration Process**_____
    Duration: Forty-five seconds to four minutes
    * May Include Process #15_____

11. **Love and Light Process**_____
    Duration: Two to six minutes_____

12. **Frequency Stabilization Process**_____
    Duration: Sixty seconds

13. **The Matrix**_____
    Duration: Approximately six minutes

14. **The Conduit of Light Process**_____
    Duration: Two to six minutes_____

15. **Dynamic of Harmony and Well-being**_____
    Duration: One to four minutes

* *See page 123 for explanation.*

APPENDIX F

Environmental Project Worksheet

Date: _____

Session: #_____

Follow-up Date: _____

Project: _____ *Amount of light & symbol:* _____

Description of Environment: _____
_____
_____

Intention: _____
_____
_____

Co-Creative Partners Present: _____
_____
_____

Processes called for (Also note duration) _____
_____
_____

APPENDIX G

Light and Symbols Chart

If the **Light is a "1,"** then the symbol to be used will be a flat **Triangle**. This **Triangle** will be placed into the "heart" of the property.

If the **Light is a "2,"** then the symbol to be used will be a **Tetrahedron**. The **Tetrahedron** will be placed into the "heart" of the property.

If the **Light is a "3,"** then the symbol to be used will be a **Cube**. The **Cube** will be placed into the "heart" of the property.

If the **Light is a "4,"** then the symbol to be used will be a **Dodecahedron**. The **Dodecahedron** will be placed into the "heart" of the property.

None of these four symbols will spin.

If the **Light is a "5,"** then the symbol to be used is a **Stellated Icosahedron**. The **Stellated Icosahedron** will be placed into the "heart" of the property.

If the **Light is a "6,"** then the symbol to be used is a **Stellated Dodecahedron**. The **Stellated Dodecahedron** will be placed into the "heart" of the property.

If the **Light is a "7,"** then the symbol to be used is a **Great Stellated Icosahedron**. The **Great Stellated Icosahedron** will be placed into the "heart" of the property.

If the **Light is an "8,"** then the symbol to be used is a **Stellated Octahedron**. The **Stellated Octahedron** will be placed into the "heart" of the property.

If the **Light is a "9,"** then the symbol to be used is a **Great Stellated Dodecahedron**. The **Great Stellated Dodecahedron** will be placed into the "heart" of the property.

If the **Light is a "10,"** then the symbol to be used is a **Star Tetrahedron**. The **Star Tetrahedron** will be placed into the "heart" of the property.

If the **Light is an "11,"** then the symbol to be used is a **Star Icosahedron**. The **Star Icosahedron** will be placed into the "heart" of the property.

If the **Light is a "12,"** then the symbol to be used is a **Star Icosidodecahedron**. The **Star Icosidodecahedron** will be placed into the "heart" of the property.

All eight of these symbols will spin in a counter-clockwise direction when inserted into the "heart" of the property.

Illustrations for Five Geometric Symbols

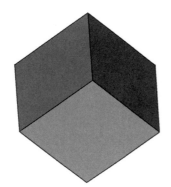

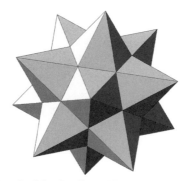

Symbol 1: Cube

Symbol 2: Stellated Dodecahedron

Symbol 3: Star Icosahedron

Symbol 4: Tetrahedron

Symbol 5: Dodecahedron

How to Contact Us

For more information about the author, seminars, or products please visit us on the Web at: www.AwakenedEarth.com

or write us at:

Masters House Press
P.O. Box 5414
Asheville, NC 28813

E-mail: info@AwakenedEarth.com

For a free offering from The Awakened Earth Masters on the current global disturbances we invite you to the Awakened Earth website. There you will find information on upcoming events, certification trainings, and workshop offerings to help you participate in this timely new movement to bring health and sustainability to the planet.

Simply go to :

www.AwakenedEarth.com

to access our website

or:

www.AwakenedEarth.com/bonus

to receive free offering